The Chancellors' Tales

THE LONDON SCHOOL
OF ECONOMICS AND
POLITICAL SCIENCE ■

LSE is small, specialist and one of the most international universities in the world. Founded in 1895 by Fabians Beatrice and Sidney Webb, LSE aims to be a laboratory of the social sciences, a place where ideas are developed, analysed, evaluated and disseminated around the globe.

LSE, based in the heart of London, has a cosmopolitan student body of around 7,800 full-time students and 750 part-time students. Of these, about 36 per cent come from the UK, 17 per cent from other European Union countries, and 47 per cent from more than 110 countries around the world. There are over 1,700 full-time members of staff. A total of 44 per cent are from countries outside the UK. LSE staff advise governments, serve on Royal Commissions, public bodies and government inquiries, and are seconded to national and international organizations.

In the most recent national research assessment in the UK, LSE came second after Cambridge for the quality of its research – and top if only the social sciences are taken into account. In the *THES*'s 2004 world rankings, LSE was top of the UK institutions and second in the world for the social sciences, behind Harvard. While always international since its foundation, the School has recently begun to develop distinctive programmes in partnership with select higher education institutions across the world, including Sciences Po in Paris and Columbia University in New York, to offer students a truly global education.

Thirteen Nobel Prize winners in economics, peace and literature have been either LSE staff or alumni. Many world leaders have also studied at the school and there are around 60 LSE alumni in the UK Houses of Parliament.

Director: Howard Davies

LSE
Houghton Street
London WC2 2AE
Tel: +44 (0)20 7405 7686
www.lse.ac.uk

The Chancellors' Tales

Managing the British Economy

Edited by
Howard Davies

polity

Individual chapters copyright © their authors; this collection
© Polity Press 2006

First published in 2006 by Polity Press

Polity Press
65 Bridge Street
Cambridge CB2 1UR, UK

Polity Press
350 Main Street
Malden, MA 02148, USA

ISBN-10: 0-7456-3884-8
ISBN-13: 978-07456-3884-3
ISBN-10: 0-7456-3885-6 (pb)
ISBN-13: 978-07456-3885-0 (pb)

A catalogue record for this book is available from the British Library.

Typeset in 11 pt 14 Sabon
by Servis Filmsetting Ltd, Manchester
Printed and bound in Great Britain by MPG Books Ltd, Bodmin, Cornwall

The publisher has used its best endeavours to ensure that the URLs for
external websites referred to in this book are correct and active at the time
of going to press. However, the publisher has no responsibility for the
websites and can make no guarantee that a site will remain live or that the
content is or will remain appropriate.

Every effort has been made to trace all copyright holders, but if any have
been inadvertently overlooked the publishers will be pleased to include any
necessary credits in any subsequent reprint or edition.

For further information on Polity, visit our website: www.polity.co.uk

Contents

Foreword

Chancellors of the Exchequer, like orchestral conductors, seem to live a long time. In the case of conductors, their longevity is usually attributed to the aerobic exercise their work involves. There is no obvious explanation for the durability of chancellors: one might have thought that overseeing the British economy in the late twentieth century was a ticket to an early grave. Yet, at the end of 2004, all chancellors back to 1974 were still with us – and all still able to give a powerful account of their period in office (see Appendix).

Five of them accepted an invitation to explain themselves, to an audience of faculty, students and others at the London School of Economics.[1] Sadly, Jim Callaghan, who could have taken the story back to 1964, was unable to take part. He declined graciously, citing ill health. Callaghan died early in 2005. John Major also asked to be excused, on the grounds that his occupation of 11 Downing Street had been brief. That is true, of course, and during his time interest rates were never

raised. Yet his decision to put sterling into the Exchange
Rate Mechanism in October 1990 shaped Acts 3 and 4
of this five-act play, and the consequences of that decision still exert a decisive influence on British attitudes to
the euro.

Four of the five chancellors who spoke – Denis Healey,
Geoffrey Howe, Nigel Lawson and Norman Lamont –
have already published memoirs of their time in office.[2]
No doubt Kenneth Clarke will do so one day. Those
memoirs, particularly Nigel Lawson's impressive tome,
which includes considerable detail on the economic
policy debates of the time, will remain essential reading
for students of the UK economy and politics in the last
quarter of the twentieth century. But this collection of
lectures, delivered with the benefit of a longer perspective, and perhaps without the *apologia pro vita sua*
dimension of the political memoir, provides a succinct
assessment of the crucial issues each chancellor faced. It
shows how the economic legacy of one became a mill-
stone – or a springboard – for the next.

The lectures also give a flavour of just what the
Treasury and its people were like at that time. I worked
in Great George Street under Healey, Howe and Lawson,
observed the Treasury closely from the vantage point of
the CBI when Norman Lamont was chancellor, and was
given a front-row seat in 'the Ken and Eddie show', when
Clarke appointed me as deputy governor of the Bank of
England. The Treasury described here, with all its warts
and beauty spots on display, is indeed the one I knew.

The styles of the five pieces are very different. They
reflect in part the different personalities of the men, but

also the nature of the problems they faced and the approach they took to them.

Denis Healey's reflections are atmospheric, gossipy and personal. Perhaps, thirty years on, the personalities of the time loom larger in the memory than the details of each public expenditure round. But Healey's contribution also accurately reflects the greater need at that time to achieve policy ends by persuasion. An approach to controlling inflation built on prices and incomes policies stood or fell by the chancellor's ability to bring the key trade union leaders along. Trade unions are barely mentioned by the other four, a revealing commentary on the declining importance of organized labour during the period.

Geoffrey Howe focuses close attention on what he still sees as the defining moment of his chancellorship: confrontation with the massed ranks of the economics profession after the 1981 budget, whose rigour caused 90 per cent of the profession in the UK to catch its collective breath; 364 economists wrote to *The Times*, rejecting his policy. Howe clearly thinks, two decades later, that he has had the better of the argument. Others remain to be convinced.

Nigel Lawson centres on the Mais Lecture of 1984 in which he proposed his celebrated redefinition of the respective roles of macro- and micro-economic policies. In future, he argued, we would see macro-policy as the tool to control inflation, while micro-policy would be used to promote growth and employment. He argues that this revised formulation has become the new orthodoxy. (Gordon Brown does not wholly agree –

but it is noteworthy that his own Mais Lecture, in 1999, made extensive reference to Lawson's 1984 version.)

Norman Lamont took office after John Major's fateful decision to put sterling into the ERM. He inevitably gives most prominence to the events of the summer of 1992, leading to our ignominious departure from the mechanism on 16 September, and on the subsequent rapid reconstruction of a policy framework, some of whose elements, notably the inflation target, survive to this day.

Kenneth Clarke, who inherited Lamont's new framework in 1993, sees his biggest achievement as the reassertion of control over the public finances. He is not kind to his predecessor's record on public spending. But he gives full weight, too, to the further development of the monetary policy framework which he pushed forward and, inevitably, gives his own trenchant views on the euro in particular, and Britain's European engagement in general.

Together with the transcripts of the question and answer sessions, which follow the lectures and in each case raise important additional issues, these lectures provide a fascinating insight into economic policy-making in Britain from 1974 to 1997 and beyond.

Note

1   The speeches and question and answer sessions took place at the London School of Economics and Political Science on the following dates:

Foreword

Lord Healey of Riddlesden: Why the Treasury is so Difficult, 28 October 2004

Lord Howe of Aberavon: Can 364 Economists all be wrong? 9 November 2004

Lord Lawson of Blaby: Changing the Consensus, 15 November 2004

Lord Lamont of Lerwick: Out of the Ashes, 23 November 2004

Kenneth Clarke MP: The Quest for the Holy Grail: Low Inflation and Growth, 29 November 2004.

2　Denis Healey, *The Time of my Life*. London: Michael Joseph, 1989; Geoffrey Howe, *Conflict of Loyalty*. London: Macmillan, 1994; Nigel Lawson, *The View from No. 11: Memoirs of a Tory Radical*. London: Bantam, 1992; Norman Lamont, *In Office: The Chancellor's Story*. London: Little, Brown, 1999.

1

Introduction

Howard Davies[1]

This first section provides a chronological review of the period described in the chancellors' lectures. The second draws out a number of themes which emerge from all five contributions.

Chronology

The conventional story of Britain's economic perform-ance over the last forty years is easily told. While the economy continued to grow through the 1950s and 1960s it became clear that our economic performance, relative to that of other comparable developed countries, was deteriorating. Both West Germany and France recovered more rapidly after the Second World War, and continued to grow more quickly. French GDP per head in fact overtook Britain's in 1975 and the West Germans became, on average, wealthier than the British the following year (figure 1.1).

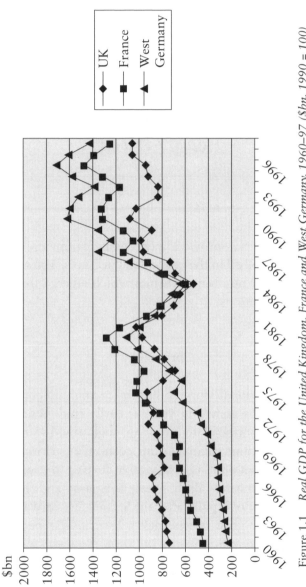

Figure 1.1 *Real GDP for the United Kingdom, France and West Germany, 1960–97 ($bn, 1990 = 100)*
Sources: IMF and Arbeitskreis.

Introduction

This poor growth record was associated in the 1960s with the recurrent weakness of sterling. Repeated balance of payments crises thwarted government attempts to stimulate growth, as domestic production failed to respond to increased demand and imports ballooned. Productivity growth in the UK fell well behind the rates achieved in the US and the major Continental European economies. In the 1960s, too, inflation began to become a problem, seen at the time to be largely the result of over- powerful and short-sighted unions bidding up wages. The public finances also deteriorated, with public borrowing on a rising trend in real terms. By 1964 public expenditure accounted for 39 per cent of GDP, up from 27 per cent in 1951.

The central economic policy-making departments suffered significant reputational damage from this lengthy period of poor relative performance. The Treasury was widely seen as a department run by well-meaning amateurs, lacking in imagination and, worse, in determination. Many thought it had become too strongly focused on finance, rather than on the performance of the economy as a whole. The Bank of England, nationalized in 1946, was seen as stuffy and out of touch, excessively concerned with the plight of sterling and with the fortunes of financial markets and firms in the City of London, rather than with the performance of the real economy.

1964–1970

After Labour's election victory of October 1964 Harold Wilson attempted to add a long-term focus to policy-making with the creation of the Department of Economic Affairs (DEA). Led by George Brown, a charismatic, if volatile, politician, its brief was to provide challenge and stimulus to the Treasury, where James Callaghan became Wilson's first chancellor of the Exchequer.

This dual structure was doomed to failure, a failure which was well chronicled by one of its temporary employees, Sir Samuel Brittan, subsequently a distinguished economic commentator on the *Financial Times*.[2] But in creating the Department of Economic Affairs Wilson could be said only to have been copying the model which applies in many other European countries, where there are typically two separate ministries, of economic affairs and finance, respectively.

While George Brown struggled to find a role for the DEA, Callaghan struggled with the financial markets – or the 'gnomes of Zurich', as currency speculators were colourfully dubbed by Wilson. His entire period of office was dominated by one economic problem: sterling. The exchange rate of around $2.80 to the pound had been maintained since 1949. Wilson staked the reputation of the new government on maintaining it, though made much of his difficult inheritance from the Conservatives, with a balance of payments current account deficit in 1964 of over £300 million – 1 per cent of GDP. At the time, this seemed an alarming statistic.

Most commentators, and more importantly most foreign exchange traders, eventually came to the view that the fixed dollar exchange rate was not sustainable, and in due course the government itself concluded that the cost of trying to maintain it was too high. In November 1967 the existing parity was abandoned and sterling was devalued by 14 per cent (figure 1.2). Harold Wilson famously asserted that 'the pound in your pocket' had not lost value at home, and argued that devaluation would allow Britain to 'break from the straitjacket' of boom and bust economics. But the episode was the first in a series of debacles which, by the end of the 1970, left Labour with a reputation for incompetence in economic management. This strongly influenced the approach taken by Tony Blair and Gordon Brown in 1997, particularly the decision to grant interest rate independence to the Bank of England.

James Callaghan took the view that, whatever the merits of the decision to devalue, his own credibility had been damaged, and resigned. (In his lecture Norman Lamont explains why he took a different view after sterling's departure from the ERM twenty-five years later.) Callaghan was replaced by Roy Jenkins, a man of great intellect and even greater erudition. Jenkins's political reputation now rests more on his period as president of the European Commission and as one of the four founders of the Social Democratic Party. But his tenure as chancellor of the Exchequer was relatively successful. Devaluation relaxed one policy constraint and gave exporters a significant boost to competitiveness. His early deflationary budgets pushed the public sector towards surplus. Growth picked up, and in 1970 economic conditions looked favourable for another Labour election victory. Jenkins's last budget in 1970 disappointed popular expectations, however, and was seen as a factor contributing to Wilson's defeat.

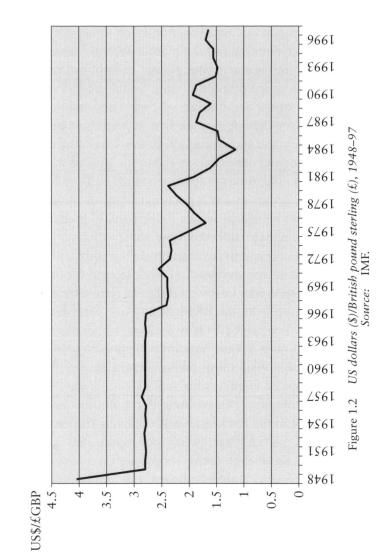

Figure 1.2   US dollars ($)/British pound sterling (£), 1948–97

Source: IMF.

Introduction

In retrospect, it may also be argued that neither Callaghan nor Jenkins did much to address the structural rigidities in the economy. The Labour government's attempts to provide a new legal framework to constrain the power of the trade unions – Barbara Castle's 'In Place of Strife' proposals – were abandoned in the face of opposition from the Labour movement. Public spending had continued on its upward trend and, in spite of the 1967 devaluation, by 1970 the balance of payments deficit was again growing.

1970–1974

In 1970, Edward Heath's new Conservative government was as determined to address the causes of Britain's sub-par economic performance as Harold Wilson's had been. Once again, the government's efforts were thwarted. Although the new government proclaimed that 'lame duck' firms would no longer be supported by the public purse, the failure of Rolls-Royce in 1971 tested that policy to destruction. And an attempt to promote above-trend growth resulted in a rapid up-tick in inflation, as the supply side failed to respond.

Iain Macleod was Heath's first popular choice as chancellor of the Exchequer. Unfortunately, he was taken ill shortly after his appointment and died a few weeks later, to the great disappointment of those who believed his outstanding intellect would have brought greater rigour and discipline to economic policy-making. His replacement, Anthony Barber, went on later in his career to become a distinguished chairman of Standard Chartered Bank. But his tenure at the Treasury was less successful. Though growth accelerated in 1972 and 1973, it was no more sustainable than past spurts had been. The first major oil price rise in 1973 was an unhelpful addition to the mix. So the 'Barber boom' ended in tears and rising inflation, as other similar episodes had done before it.

The Heath government lost office after the latest in a series of confrontations between the government and the National Union of Miners. After failing to resist NUM demands through a series of increasingly desperate expedients, notably a three-day week in which workplaces were not supplied with power on the other two weekdays, Heath sought a new mandate from the electorate. He failed to secure one. The 'Who governs Britain?' election of February 1974 brought Harold Wilson back into office, though without an overall majority in Parliament. Even the second 1974 election, in October, left Labour with a majority in Parliament of only four seats, a fragile basis on which to take difficult or controversial decisions.

1974–1979

Such was the unpromising background against which Denis Healey, the first of the five chancellors who appear in this volume, took office.

Healey had many strengths, which made him a plausible, even compelling choice as the Prime Minister's right-hand man. Neither Callaghan nor Jenkins would have welcomed reappointment to the Treasury: Healey was clearly the third heavyweight in the party. His long tenure at the Ministry of Defence, where he served for the whole of Wilson's first term, gave him vital experience in the Cabinet as the head of a major spending department. His intellectual ability to engage with Treasury officials was not in doubt. On the other hand, as a man perceived now to be on Labour's right wing (after a youthful flirtation with the Communist Party), he could expect no personal favours from the trade unions, especially in the public sector.

His period of office hinged on the painful year of 1976. Before then, Healey pursued an expansionist policy, in an attempt to promote recovery from the trauma of the Three-Day Week. In two so-called mini-budgets in July and November 1974 he increased food subsidies, reduced VAT and announced large rises in government aid to industry.

By the following year this strategy was already looking highly risky, and both public expenditure cuts and tax increases were announced. These measures proved insufficient to correct a worsening fiscal position.

Sterling's continued weakness, and the need for external finance, pushed the UK into the hands of the IMF in 1976 – a second episode which damaged Labour's reputation for economic competence. Photographs of an IMF delegation entering Treasury Chambers were a vivid symbol of Britain's economic plight. The IMF's role, surely, was to knock sense into governments in developing countries such as Argentina or Mexico, lacking the political maturity to solve their own problems unaided, not to bail out one of its founding fathers?

But by 1976 it seemed that only external pressure could induce British governments to take the tough decisions needed to preserve financial stability.

Denis Healey argues in his contribution that, in fact, the government did not need to go cap in hand to the IMF in 1976. Had the public spending forecasts been more accurate, he says, there would have been no need to seek IMF support. That may be so, but we may presume that no government would wish to operate within the margin of forecasting error, and the requirement to repay a loan to the Bank of International Settlements in Basel forced the government into the hands of the Fund.

After the IMF visitations, and the subsequent fiscal tightening, the position improved significantly. A supplementary budget in December 1976 announced large cuts in public expenditure plans and the sale by the government of some of its BP shareholding: this was a precursor of the privatizations to follow in the 1980s, though at the time it was not seen as such.

The shock of the threat of national bankruptcy, as it was perceived, created conditions in which the unions were prepared to agree more moderate wage rises, and inflation fell back, from a peak of 24 per cent in 1975 to 'only' 8 per cent in 1978 (figure 1.3). It seemed possible that Labour might win an election in the autumn of 1978, but Prime Minister Callaghan, who had replaced Wilson in 1976, cautiously decided to wait until the spring of the following year before going to the country.

It proved a decisive error of judgement. The winter of 1978–9, still present in public consciousness as the 'Winter of Discontent', was disastrous for the

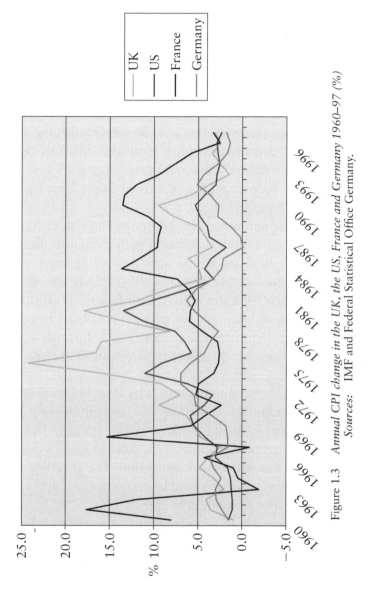

Figure 1.3   *Annual CPI change in the UK, the US, France and Germany 1960–97 (%)*
Sources: IMF and Federal Statistical Office Germany.

government. A rash of industrial disputes, some official, some wildcat, left rubbish rotting in the streets and bodies unburied. Healey acknowledges here that his own misjudgement played a part in precipitating the crisis. In an attempt to bring inflation down further he sought to reach agreement with the unions on a guideline of 5 per cent for wage increases. Union leaders were unwilling, or unable, to deliver a number that low. Had Healey pitched for something less ambitious, large-scale strikes might have been averted, and Labour might have been re-elected in May 1979.

But it was not to be. The Winter of Discontent crystallized a mood of dissatisfaction with the government, and indeed with its whole approach to steering the economy. Though the Treasury did begin to monitor monetary growth more closely than before, even after the IMF episode anti-inflation policy was essentially seen as the control of prices and incomes, with the latter – as it seemed – under the effective direction of the trade unions.

In the 1979 election campaign, Mrs Thatcher promised a different approach. No more 'beer and sandwiches' at 10 Downing Street with union bosses (though Denis Healey tells us that, if you really wanted to strike a deal, *goujons de sole* had to be on the menu). The government would govern, inflation would be conquered at last, taxes and public spending would be cut.

But although the direction of change was well signalled in the Conservative manifesto of 1979, few expected the new approach to economic policy to prove as radical a break with the past as it turned out to be.

Introduction

1979–1983

Few chancellors have reached the Treasury as well pre-pared as Geoffrey Howe when he took over in May 1979. As he explains, the Conservative Party in opposition had devoted considerable time and energy to a fundamental review of the role of government in economic policy. The seminal published text – too little read, perhaps, when it appeared in October 1977 – was a policy paper entitled *The Right Approach to the Economy*.[3] Geoffrey Howe was one of the authors, Keith Joseph was another.

It set the scene for an approach to controlling inflation based on a targeted reduction in monetary growth, building on the work of Milton Friedman and other monetary economists in the US and the UK – though 'monetarism' (a term which Geoffrey Howe is reluctant to adopt) was a minority enthusiasm in the British economic community at the time.

Howe's explanation here of the origins of this new approach, and its implications, is very thorough. He also well describes the challenge to it from unsympathetic members of the economics profession: 364 economists signed a letter to *The Times* in response to Howe's 1981 budget, in which he raised taxes and cut spending at a time of recession – a sharp challenge to the tenets of Keynesian orthodoxy.

Howe claims today that his budget can now clearly be seen to have been appropriate and to have laid the foundations of the subsequent period of healthy growth with low inflation. Indeed, he argues that if it can now be faulted it is for being too lax on public spending. But at

13

the time the policy seemed both needlessly masochistic and, to many, full of contradictions.

Howe's early decisions were radical in a number of important respects. In October 1979 he announced the immediate abolition of exchange controls, a dramatic liberalization of financial markets, with positive long-term consequence for the City of London. He also pushed forward the deregulation of credit markets (which was to prove a complicating factor in future formulations of monetary policy, as credit expansion confused the messages from growth rates in the monetary aggregates).

The foundation stone of the Howe approach to macro-economic policy was the Medium Term Financial Strategy (MTFS), launched in the 1980 budget, which set a target range for sterling M3, a broad definition of the money supply which could approximately be described as notes, coins and bank deposits, plus the government's deficit, plus or minus movements on the external account. The range for £M3 growth in 1980–81 was 7 to 11 per cent – the 4 per cent band would allow for forecast error, as practical experience of operating with monetary targets was limited.

In fact, in that year £M3 grew by 18 per cent (figure 1.4). Minimum lending rate rose to 17 per cent during 1979, and though it fell back to 12 per cent by the time of the 1981 budget, by the autumn of that year rates were rising again. As a junior Treasury official in the Home Finance Division (though with the grandiloquent title of 'Principal – Monetary Policy'), I well recall drafting parliamentary answers in 1981 which sought to explain why, although £M3 growth was running at close

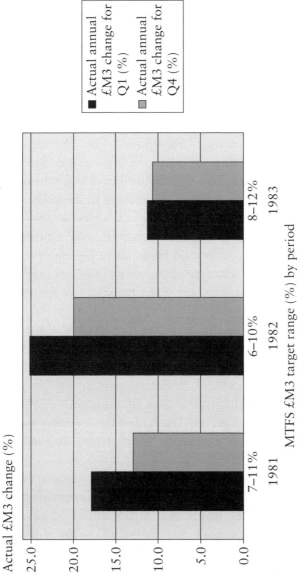

Figure 1.4 *MTFS £M3 target ranges and actual growth rates (on adjusted figures), 1980–83 (%)*
Sources: Bank of England and Her Majesty's Treasury.

to twice the top of the target range, the policy framework nonetheless remained intact. The draftsman's ingenuity was sorely taxed.

The 'misbehaviour' of £M3 was not wholly understood at the time. One explanation is that it was the delayed-action consequence of the ending of quantitative restrictions on bank balance sheets during the 1970s. A further factor was that, since a large proportion of £M3 deposits are interest-bearing, interest rate rises could have the perverse effect of attracting money into £M3, thus inflating the aggregate rather than reducing it. Another, semi-serious argument was proposed by Charles Goodhart, at the time a Bank of England economist, now a professor at the London School of Economics. Goodhart's Law has it that any monetary aggregate will alter its predicted behaviour as soon as it is given the status of an official target.

The facts show that inflation rose sharply in the first year of Mrs Thatcher's government, to a peak of 21 per cent, before falling back. Whatever the explanation, in an attempt to control monetary growth interest rates remained very high at a time of economic weakness. Sterling rose sharply as a result, and the economy passed through a severe recession, which had a particularly sharp impact on manufacturing industry. In his lecture, and the subsequent question and answer session, Howe debates the question of whether the gain justified the pain. He is in no doubt that it did: others continue to believe that the output costs in the UK of the reduction in inflation (which all accept was necessary) were higher than elsewhere because of the policy mix the government adopted. Since the counterfactual is unknown, that argument is impossible to resolve definitively.

In the aftermath of Mrs Thatcher's victory in the Falklands War of 1982, the economy played a less significant role in the 1983 election than it might otherwise have done. The Labour Party's manifesto, which reflected the views of its then leader, Michael Foot, advocated nuclear disarmament and withdrawal from NATO and the EU, giving the government many other tempting political targets at which to aim. So, even though there were still more than 3 million unemployed people in 1983, the Conservatives were re-elected with another large majority.

But while, in the round, the economic record of the Howe years was mixed, he was able to point to one concrete result of his tough policies: inflation had fallen back to only 3.7 per cent by the time he left the Treasury for the Foreign office. The UK was no longer an outlier in terms of inflation performance among the major industrialized nations (figure 1.5).

Margaret Thatcher, to no one's surprise, named Nigel Lawson, who had been financial secretary to the Treasurey at the time of the elaboration of the MTFS and the 1981 budget, as his successor.

1983–1990

Lawson had subsequently spent a brief period as secretary of state for energy, but was the logical choice to maintain the policy line set by his predecessor. Like all the

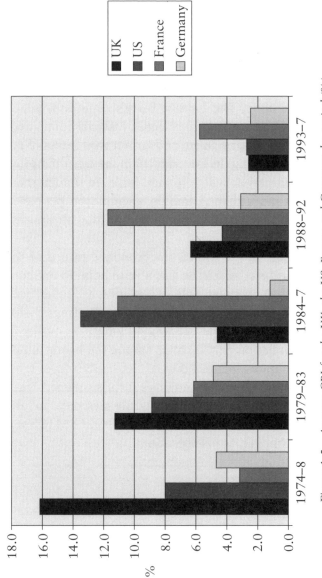

Figure 1.5   *Average CPI for the UK, the US, France and Germany, by period (%)*
Sources: IMF and Federal Statistical Office Germany.

chancellors featured here, Lawson was not a professional economist, but he was perhaps the one who felt most comfortable engaging in debate with economists. He had been city editor of the *Sunday Telegraph*, as well as editor of *The Spectator*, and relished intellectual argument.

The Lawson years in the Treasury formed, to coin a football phrase, a game of two halves. Although sterling staged one of its worrying collapses in 1984–5, falling to a record low of $1.03 (in February 1985), the first four years of his time at the Treasury were enviably smooth and successful. Inflation remained low, averaging 4.5 per cent a year throughout the 1983–7 parliament, and unemployment gradually fell. Confidence in the maintenance of low inflation was backed by the government's success in the long miners' strike of 1984–5, a sharp contrast with the Heath years.

Lawson's own reputation grew as the economy expanded, so that in 1988 Mrs Thatcher famously described her chancellor as 'unassailable'. As he argues here, his 1984 Mais Lecture had set out a new approach to economic policy-making. He sums up that new approach as follows: 'instead of seeking to use macro-economic policy . . . to promote growth and employment, and micro-economic policy (of which prices and incomes policy was the central component) to suppress inflation, we should do precisely the reverse. That is to say, the government of the day should direct macro-economic policy . . . to suppress inflation, and micro-economic policy . . . to provide all the other conditions most favourable to improved performance in terms of growth and employment.'

This reformulation proved a useful guide to the broad strategic approach the government adopted. But, beneath the surface, there were problems. The MTFS, in spite of repeated reformulations, failed to deliver a robust set of relationships between monetary growth and inflation. 'By the mid-1980s domestic monetary targeting had clearly lost . . . credibility', Lawson maintains. And by 1987 he had adopted an informal link between sterling and the Deutschmark at around DM3 to the pound, as a proxy for Exchange Rate Mechanism membership.

We then entered a troubled period in which British monetary policy was heavily influenced by external developments. Lawson believed that a period of external discipline 'would assist in the final stages of eradicating inflation and inflationary expectations'. That was the essential justification for his policy of shadowing the DM.

But it was not to be. Lawson gives his view of the reasons – a combination of policy misjudgements, when monetary conditions were loosened in 1986, and, later on, external events. In particular, after 1989, German reunification created inflationary pressures in Germany, requiring higher interest rates to choke them off. This was highly uncomfortable for countries, like the UK and Italy, where economic conditions pointed to the need for lower rates to counter recession.

The consequences of this combination of circumstances for the British economy were severe. Inflation began to rise once again in 1988, and reached a peak of 9.5 per cent in 1990. Interest rates rose sharply. The economy moved into recession (figure 1.6). Lawson tried and failed in 1988 to persuade the Prime Minister to give the Bank of England independence in setting interest rates. Sterling remained outside the ERM, again owing to prime ministerial opposition.

By this time relations between Mrs Thatcher and her two key lieutenants, Howe and Lawson, had deteriorated sharply, largely on the issue of European policy, though her decision to reappoint Alan Walters – a man who made no secret of his disagreements with Lawson – as her economic adviser in 10 Downing Street did not help relations with the Treasury. In October 1989 Lawson concluded that his position was untenable and resigned, propelling John Major into the chancellor's office. Twelve months later, on 1 November 1990, Geoffrey Howe left the government, and Mrs Thatcher herself was forced out of office three weeks afterwards. She was succeeded, after a contested election, by her recently appointed chancellor.

Major's stay in 11 Downing Street was brief, but one momentous decision with huge long-term ramifications was made: Britain joined the ERM on 8 October 1990, at a central rate of DM2.95 to the pound. Her resolve weakened by the political pressure mounting on her increasingly strident anti-European policy, Margaret Thatcher had conceded. On the day, the stock market rose, and sterling moved towards the top of its permitted 6 per cent fluctuation band around the central rate. Business reactions were generally positive.

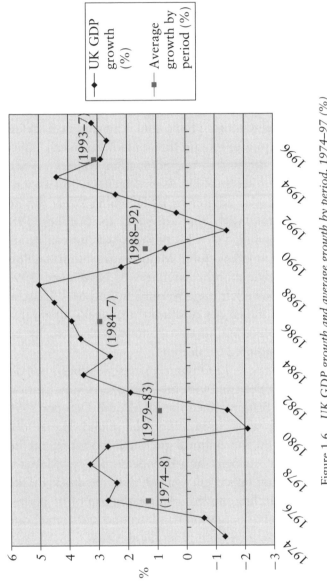

Figure 1.6   UK GDP growth and average growth by period, 1974–97 (%)
Source: Office for National Statistics.

Introduction

1990–1993

Joining the ERM certainly resolved the problem which had come to preoccupy Nigel Lawson: the UK's anti-inflation policy had found a new anchor. And the ERM certainly helped engineer a rapid reduction in inflation. When John Major inserted sterling into the ERM the inflation rate was just under 10 per cent. When the UK was unceremoniously ejected on 16 September 1992, it was below 4 per cent.

There were, however, two related problems. First, although interest rates fell during the UK's time in the ERM, from 14 per cent to 10 per cent (if one excepts the temporary spike on the last day – 16 September), they were certainly higher than was appropriate, given the depressed state of the economy. The UK experienced a sharp recession in the early 1990s, one which hit manufacturing particularly hard: from peak to trough, industrial production declined by 3 per cent. Yet the ERM constraint severely restricted the authorities' ability to respond to this weakness. Reunification created very different conditions in Germany. The Germans needed relatively high rates to offset the inflationary consequences of reunification, especially in view of Helmut Kohl's essentially political decision to convert Ostmarks to Deutschmarks at 1 to 1.

The other, linked, problem was that, during the UK's period of membership, the foreign exchange markets came to believe that sterling's central rate had been set too high at entry. In retrospect we can see that, although it fell quite sharply on the UK's exit from the ERM, the pound later recovered and traded around or above the DM2.95 rate for most of the next decade.

Norman Lamont, who took office in November 1990, in John Major's first administration, may reasonably consider himself to be one of the unluckiest chancellors of the post-war period. He inherited a policy from his predecessor which proved to be unsustainable. Unfortunately, that predecessor was now his boss, and had left no Plan B in the bottom drawer in the event that it proved impossible to sustain sterling's position.

In his contribution to this collection Lamont explains the crisis of September 1992 in entertaining detail, and with a remarkable lack of rancour. He reminds us that the ERM experienced a generalized crisis in the summer of 1992. A number of other currencies, from the Finnish markka to the Italian lira, also fell out of the mechanism. He does not, however, attempt to disguise the magnitude of the policy failure which 16 September – 'Black Wednesday' – represented.

By the evening of Black Wednesday, in spite of a 2 per cent interest rate rise during the day, and the threat of 3 per cent more, sterling had been ejected from the ERM and the government's economic policy was in ruins. At the time, I was director-general of the CBI. Coincidentally, the CBI's Governing Council met on the same day. The mood among the CBI politburo was sombre. Messengers brought news of the rate rises to the platform as we debated some inconsequential policy paper. It was clear that the ERM game, which the CBI had supported, was up. By the evening, there was no anti-inflation strategy, no policy anchor. Furthermore, the monetary policy approaches adopted during the 1980s were no longer available. The government had itself acknowledged that its monetary targets had not proved to be satisfactory guides to policy, hence the decision to target the exchange rate.

These were the unpromising circumstances in which the inflation target was born. Lamont himself oversaw the process of creating a new framework: its intellectual parentage may owe more to the contributions of Terry Burns and Alan Budd at the Treasury, and of Mervyn King, who had recently joined the Bank of England from the London School of Economics as its chief economist.

The outcome of their work was set out in the unusual format of a letter to the then Chair of the Treasury Select Committee, drafted by Andrew Turnbull, subsequently Permanent Secretary to the Treasury and Secretary to the Cabinet.[4] John Watts MP, by virtue of his position at the crucial moment, thus earns himself a permanent footnote in the history of British economic policy.

The letter explained that, in future, the government would set an inflation target, which would guide its monetary policy. Sterling would be allowed to float. The Bank of England would publish a quarterly inflation report, setting out its own independent view of inflationary conditions, and there would be regular monthly meetings between the chancellor and the governor at which interest rate decisions would be made. The outcomes of those meetings, whether or not rates were changed, would be publicly announced. This was half a step towards central bank independence. Lamont explains here that he would have liked to go further but, once again, Prime Minister Major, like Thatcher before him, rejected his Chancellor's advice that full operational independence for the Bank would bolster market credibility.

Lamont's other signal contribution to the re-establishment of a coherent policy was the budget of 1993, which increased taxes sharply, an echo of the 1981 Howe budget. As that budget had been, it was hugely unpopular at the time, but – Lamont argues with some justification – it created the basis for the sound fiscal position which Labour inherited four years later.

Lamont himself did not stay at the Treasury long enough to discover whether his new inflation target regime would gain the confidence of the markets and prove a stable basis for interest rate decisions. Though his offer to resign on Black Wednesday had been declined, he was removed from office by John Major in May 1993 and returned to the backbenches. Lamont clearly resented both the timing and the manner of his dismissal. Kenneth Clarke was appointed in his place, moving over from the Home Office.

1993–1997

Clarke had already brought his no-nonsense, pugnacious, beer and cigar approach to a succession of ministerial posts, earning a reputation as an impressive parliamentary performer and a man not afraid to take on vested interests. The Treasury, however, was a different type of challenge, and Clarke had little if any background in economics. But, as he says, he had one trump card, which more or less guaranteed him a lengthy period in office: 'if a prime minister sacks a chancellor, he cannot sack a second.'

In spite of the work Lamont and his advisers had done in the autumn of 1992, and in spite of the fact that the economy had been recovering since the spring of that year, the mood remained one of crisis. Indeed Clarke is less than flattering about the fiscal position he inherited from his predecessor, noting that his own first budget included 'the largest increase in the burden of taxation in any budget delivered by any chancellor since the war'.

But in terms of macro-economic policy formulation, Clarke's contribution was to push the interest rate-setting process further towards a central bank independence regime. He increased the Bank's influence in two important ways. First, he says he abandoned the Treasury practice of 'commenting on' the draft of the Bank's inflation report, so that in future the Bank could give its unvarnished view of inflationary conditions, and the probability of meeting the inflation target with current interest rates. Second, and more important, he decided to publish the minutes of the monthly meetings between the chancellor and the governor, and the advice the latter gave each month. (A third contribution – more memorable, albeit less significant in policy terms – was to describe the monthly encounter with the Bank as 'the Ken and Eddie Show'.) These refinements buttressed the model put in place by Lamont.

The published minutes did in due course reveal that a difference of view on interest rates had opened up between Ken and Eddie as the 1997 election approached. Much was made of this difference at the time, perhaps because of the novelty for the media of being given a glimpse of internal policy debates. But, by the time of the 1997 election, the gap was no wider than a quarter of 1 per cent. Unsurprisingly, the Governor was the one arguing for slightly higher rates. As deputy governor by this time, I sat beside him trying to look suitably determined, nodding when necessary as strategically placed backbenchers now do when ministers' speeches are televised.

In terms of economic performance and inflation, the Clarke years were very successful. GDP growth averaged just over 3 per cent over the four years of his chancellorship, and inflation just below 3 per cent. But even this comforting record did little to overcome the impact of Black Wednesday in the popular mind. The Conservatives' reputation for competent economic management had been damaged and was no longer a trump card in electoral terms. Furthermore, Gordon Brown committed Labour, if elected, to maintaining Clarke's tight spending plans for the first two years. As Geoffrey Howe says in answer to a question, 'until then [1997] I had been terrified that Labour spokesmen might mean what they were saying. My only fear from then on was that they might *not* mean what they were saying.'

The electorate were prepared to give Labour the benefit of the doubt, and in spite of the impressive economic recovery Gordon Brown replaced Kenneth Clarke as chancellor, under Prime Minister Tony Blair, in May 1997.

Introduction

1997 onwards

Brown made high-profile campaign commitments to maintain the Conservatives' spending plans, but while in opposition he had said little about monetary policy, except to commit, in very general terms, to the maintenance of low inflation. Attempts, both in public and in private, to induce Labour to show its hand on Economic and Monetary Union or the role of the Bank of England were not successful.

So the announcement, just days after the election, that the Bank would in future be set an inflation target by the government, and be given the freedom to set interest rates without political interference, came as a surprise. Furthermore, it emerged that in opposition Labour had prepared a detailed plan for a new Monetary Policy Committee (MPC) of nine members, including four from outside the Bank, which would determine rates at monthly meetings, publishing detailed minutes and the votes of individual members on each occasion. Ed Balls, Gordon Brown's economic adviser in opposition and in government, surprised officials by producing a worked-through scheme on his first day in Treasury Chambers.

While the precise formulation of policy and the details of the new MPC were original, the framework owes something to the New Zealand experience, in that the Bank of England is 'instrument independent' but also 'target-dependent', since the desired inflation rate is set by the government. Both the Federal Reserve and the European Central Bank have the responsibility of determining their own definition of price stability. While inflation targeting is growing in popularity around the world – more than twenty countries now operate such a regime – there is no consensus on the relative merits of instrument or target independence for the Central Bank. The superiority of a symmetrical target, as operated in London but not in Frankfurt, is increasingly acknowledged, however. The monetary authority should not have a legislated bias in favour of a rate below the declared target.

A further, significant element of the new arrangements was the removal from the Bank of England of other responsibilities which might conflict with, or create risks for, the monetary policy objective. So the responsibility for issuing government debt passed to a new Debt Management Office, and for banking supervision to a new integrated financial regulator, the Financial Services Authority. (As the Bank's deputy governor when those new arrangements were announced, I was invited to establish and chair the new Authority, which I did until late 2003.)

The UK inflation target was set initially at 2.5 per cent, with a tolerated band of plus or minus 1 per cent. If inflation strayed outside that band, the governor would be obliged to write a letter of explanation to the chancellor. (The central rate was lowered to 2 per cent, and the measurement basis was changed slightly, from the Retail Price Index to a new Consumer Prices Index, on 9 June 2003).

The new regime quickly gained market confidence. Long-term interest rates, in spite of the improved inflation performance through the 1990s, had remained around

1.5 per cent above equivalent German rates, a margin generally seen as a risk premium related to the UK's political control of short rates. After the May 1997 announcements that risk premium soon fell away.

Furthermore, the regime has so far proved remarkably successful in practice. In the first eight years of its operation inflation never moved outside the band. No gubernatorial letters have yet been written. This performance clearly owed a lot to skilful management by the governors – Eddie George until 2003, followed by Mervyn King – but the system itself had also been artfully designed, with lessons learned from the experience of the Federal Reserve, in particular.

Was this, therefore, the 'end of history' in monetary policy terms?

Norman Lamont counsels caution. 'One shouldn't', he argues, 'regard inflation targeting as an end to all argument about controlling inflation, because it still begs the question . . . what weight is to be given to monetary policy, what to asset prices, to the exchange rate?' In other words, the success of the regime still depends on a complex set of judgements, based on ambiguous evidence, made by fallible people.

For now, however, the record shows that inflation has been quiescent, and the British economy, for so long the sick man of Europe, has enjoyed thirteen years of continuous expansion. There are problems to be addressed: the low savings rate, a continuing large balance of payments deficit. But virtual price stability has been achieved, and without recourse to an external anchor, which Nigel Lawson came to think was essential. There is of course, an available anchor, if we chose to use it, in the form of the euro. But in 2006, with the prospect of a referendum on EMU membership further away than ever, following the French and Dutch rejections of the constitution, British adoption of the single currency seems a remote prospect, at best.

Themes

The unifying theme of the five lectures is the search for an approach to anti-inflation policy which would deliver monetary stability, seen by all the chancellors as a necessary if not a sufficient condition for the achievement of healthy economic growth and rising living standards. But there are other recurring motifs. In this section I review six of them and examine the way the debate on each developed over the period:

- the role of economics in policy-making
- the Treasury's role
- the relationship between the chancellor and the prime minister
- the role of the Bank of England
- the control of public spending
- Europe.

The role of economics

Of the five men, only Nigel Lawson and Norman Lamont benefited, if that is the right word, from some formal training in economics, though Lawson confesses that in his Oxford PPE course he took only two papers in economics. Geoffrey Howe claims some relevant previous experience: the others do not, and for both Lamont and Clarke their appointment to the Treasury came unexpectedly. They therefore had little or no time to prepare. Yet not one regards the absence of professional economic training as a handicap. Perhaps, as the saying goes, 'they would say that, wouldn't they?'

In one sense, we should certainly not regard this as surprising, or even remarkable. We do not expect secretaries of state for defence to have been generals or admirals. We do not expect a secretary of state for education to be a teacher, though it may be better if he or she has been to school. But it is notable that the chancellors do more than say that it is not essential to be an economist. They go out of their way to argue that economic thinking made little contribution to policy.

Healey says that economics was a positive handicap: 'The real problem, I discovered, was economics, [which] is not a science, it is a branch of social psychology.' Economic theory, he maintains, tended to be based far too much on generalizations from events that had happened two generations earlier. More seriously, perhaps, Healey believes that economists typically show 'no sense of the importance of social organizations'. Furthermore, in his view many of the arguments put to him relied on highly unreliable statistics.

Howe has a better excuse than the others to be hostile to the economics profession. The assault on his policy in a 1981 letter to *The Times* signed by 364 economists was remarkable at the time, and evidently still rankles today, even though he believes he has had the best of the argument in the intervening years.

He says he does not go so far as to argue that 'economists are uniquely *un*qualified to determine . . . the shape of government economic policy.' But while he concedes that 'some insight into economics' may be of some assistance to a politician, he asserts the value of 'the politician as intruder' into the closed world of the experts. Economists, in other words, should in his view be on tap but not on top.

Lawson shows himself to be familiar with the writings of many economists. His lecture is rich in references to Keynes, Hayek, Marshall and Adam Smith. But he is no disciple of any of them. Indeed he says he has a fundamental problem with the way the profession has developed. 'Economists . . . have mistakenly sought to dignify their calling by describing it as a science, and have increasingly chosen to add verisimilitude to this pretence by clothing their propositions in the language of science, that is to say, mathematics.' Yet he doubts if any chancellor of the Exchequer has been 'assisted in the slightest by a mathematical equation'.

We must recognize, according to Lawson, that economics is not a science, indeed it is 'more like foreign policy than it is like science, consisting as it does in seeking a rational course of action in a world of endemic uncertainty.' Only economic historians can take comfort: he believes far more economic history should be taught in our universities. (Uniquely among British universities, the LSE retains a separate economic history department.)

Neither Lamont nor Clarke devote much attention to economics. They do not share Lawson's interest in the historical and intellectual underpinnings of the policies they pursued. Clarke does criticize both the Bank of England and Treasury officials for their excessive reliance on computer models which 'just factored in what had happened when things had gone wrong before', while 'whatever goes wrong in macro-economic policy the irritating thing is that it is never the same thing twice.'

Should the economics profession be concerned to be damned with such faint praise? Economists may argue, with some justification, that even chancellors who profess to ignore economists have been influenced by their product indirectly, through the advice they receive from officials. Healey quotes Keynes's famous dictum to the effect that 'practical men, who believe themselves to be quite exempt from any intellectual influences, are usually the slaves of some defunct economist.'[5] But the unanimous view of five chancellors that formal economics has relatively little to contribute to policy-making, and is making less of a contribution as time goes by, nonetheless provides food for thought.

The Treasury's role

In the 1960s, and again in the 1990s after Black Wednesday, it was fashionable to criticize the Treasury, both for its apparent lack of technical capacity and for its excessive dominance over other departments in Whitehall. In particular, it was argued that a single department filling the roles of both a ministry of economics and a ministry of finance amounted to an excessive concentration of power. Other European countries typically divide the two roles.

As has already been explained, Harold Wilson did create a rival Department of Economic Affairs, which proved to be a short-lived experiment. The failure of that poorly planned and executed initiative queered the pitch for institutional reform, and no structural attempts to rein in the Treasury have been made for almost forty years.

All five chancellors here are unrepentant about the scope of the Treasury's responsibilities. They do not believe it is too powerful. Healey sees its ability to deliver on its policies as a crucial strength. It was on his recommendation that the Treasury regained a second Cabinet minister, when Harold Wilson elevated Joel Barnett to the Cabinet as chief secretary. All subsequent governments have kept the man (so far always a man) responsible for public spending in the Cabinet.

Lawson speaks for all his colleagues when he praises the Treasury's dual role as 'the central department, which means that the chancellor . . . has a finger in pretty well every pie the government of the day bakes.' He sees its ability to control public spending, and to involve itself in supply-side reform, as key attributes of effective policy-making. It helps 'to ensure what I would call policy coherence and what seems to be known nowadays as joined-up government.'

There is no doubt that on this point Gordon Brown would share his predecessors' views. While since 1997 the Treasury has conceded operational control of monetary policy to the Bank of England, it has involved itself more directly in many other areas of government, even those such as education and immigration which have not previously been regarded as being within the Treasury's purview. Indeed it can be argued that Brown has gone further, and turned the Treasury into a spending department in its own right.

Unusually, Brown has been responsible for a series of policy initiatives which, in the past, would have been articulated in spending departments, with the Treasury acting as the checker, the second-guesser and ultimately the paymaster. Beginning with the 'Welfare to Work' programme in Labour's first term, Gordon Brown's Treasury has launched a series of costly schemes, most notably family credits and pension credits, which make the Treasury itself responsible for the design of a sizeable chunk of public spending. Some question whether, as a result, these programmes are subject to the critical analysis which the Treasury brings to the plans of other departments.

The relationship between the chancellor and the prime minister

While the Treasury's dominance within Whitehall remains unchallenged by other departments, it is of course subject to oversight by the Prime Minister, who is also, it should be recalled, First Lord of the Treasury. In the early 1980s Margaret Thatcher was wont to make symbolic calls on Treasury divisions to underline the point. I recall a terrifying 'state visit' to the monetary policy division in 1981, at a time when £M3 was misbehaving: she appeared to hold us personally responsible.

It is not easy, though, for prime ministers to exercise effective oversight from month to month. They are heavily dependent on the Treasury itself for information and advice. While there is, by tradition, a senior Treasury official in the Number 10 private office team, he or she can be as much a conduit for Treasury thinking to reach Downing Street as a channel for prime ministerial influence on Number 11. So, in an attempt to provide themselves with an independent source of advice, prime ministers have often appointed economists to the Downing Street team, with mixed results.

All five chancellors were also asked specifically about their attitude to economic advisers based in 10 Downing Street. Here their answers vary, reflecting their personal experience. Lawson, whose departure from office was precipitated by repeated clashes with Margaret Thatcher's economic adviser, Alan Walters, is the most hostile. He concedes that private advice to the prime minister can be helpful, but 'when a personal adviser starts going public, so that it becomes unclear as to what the economic policy of the government is, then I think it is distinctly unhelpful.'

Healey thinks Harold Wilson's policy unit made little impact on policy, while Geoffrey Howe considers that 'any partly independent source of advice at Number 10 . . . is bound to make government more difficult.' Clarke is grateful that John Major's policy advisers intervened little in Treasury matters. Indeed it would seem that the unhappy experience with Alan Walters, whose personal style did not make relationships any easier, has diminished prime ministers' appetite for high-profile advisers.

Tony Blair's economic adviser, for the first eight years of his premiership, was Derek Scott, who can hardly be considered an economist of the stature of Alan Walters, though he had been an adviser to Denis Healey in the 1970s. Indeed his influence on policy was hard to discern. He complains in his memoirs[6] that he was excluded from meetings at which key decisions, on the euro for example, were taken. His account is interesting only for the proof it offers of the dominance of Gordon Brown's Treasury in all means of policy-making. So in this area the Treasury seems, for now, to have won the argument.

It may seem paradoxical that, by giving up control over one key policy instrument – interest rates – the Treasury should have strengthened its hold over others, but that is certainly the case. While, forty years ago, the Treasury seemed set to be cut down to size, today its dominance in Whitehall is greater than ever.

It may be argued, though, that an institutional analysis does not fully capture the prime minister's influence. The personal relationship between prime ministers is often uniquely close within government. The Blair–Brown axis is clearly the central feature of the Labour government. And I recall, from my time as special adviser to Nigel Lawson, that he regularly popped through the dividing door between 10 and 11 Downing Street to take Margaret Thatcher's mind on an issue of moment, whether a possible interest rate change or a public spending decision.

When this relationship breaks down, trouble ensues. Outside the scope of this book, Macmillan's sacking of Thorneycroft was a moment of crisis for his government. Harold Wilson's insertion of George Brown into the picture was notoriously unsuccessful. The breakdown of trust between Thatcher and Lawson adversely affected government policy at a crucial time. The Blair–Brown partnership has survived longest, but the periods of tension in the relationship have been threatening to the stability of the government as a whole.

It is also notable that none of the five chancellors here has moved up to the premiership, even though all were regarded, at various times, as having the calibre to do so. John Major did, but after only a short time in Number 11. A long spell at the Treasury has typically been damaging to the incumbent's chances of higher office, partly because unpopular decisions are an occupational hazard, and partly because of the structural tension between the two positions. It remains to be seen whether Gordon Brown can overcome these two obstacles.

The role of the Bank of England

There is a third leg to the stool of anti-inflation policy: the Bank of England.

The Federal Reserve in the US and the Bundesbank in Germany, have long been able to make independent decisions on short-term interest rates. During the 1980s and 1990s several other developed countries, notably the EU members planning to join the single currency, 'liberated' their central banks from political control, benefiting from enhanced policy credibility. Markets were more ready to believe that independent central banks would move interest rates in a timely manner, not as dictated by the electoral cycle. The governments' long-term borrowing rates were typically lower as a result.

Throughout the period covered by these lectures the role of the Bank was an important sub-plot, never far below the surface of events. Healey says the issue of independence did not come to prominence during his time, but it became a recurrent motif in the 1980s as other attempts to enhance policy credibility proved only partially effective. Howe, Lawson, Lamont and Clarke all claim to have been secretly in favour of the idea (though Clarke publicly opposed Gordon Brown's reforms after the 1997 election) but to have been unable to persuade their prime ministers. Both Thatcher and Major were hostile. Lawson explains that he prepared a paper recommending the change in 1988: indeed it is published in his memoirs.

Opinion among officials was divided. One Treasury permanent secretary told me he was in favour of independence for the Bank of England, 'but not *this* Bank of England'. Though all the chancellors claim to have maintained good relations with their governors, at working level tensions were evident. When I (a former Treasury man) was appointed deputy governor in 1995, the Treasury invited me in for a briefing, which amounted to a lengthy catalogue of complaints about the Bank's obsessive secrecy and its constipated working methods, whereby all issues of any substance had to be elevated to the governor's office before a view could be expressed.

Yet, in spite of this institutional distrust, successive chancellors came to see the compelling logic of a change. Why, then, were their prime ministers still not persuaded?

There is no clear answer. Margaret Thatcher was certainly influenced by the political risk of interest rate rises being imposed at politically sensitive times. The first President Bush's chances of re-election were thought to have been decisively damaged by the Federal Reserve's policies in 1992. But it may be, too, that 10 Downing Street saw the risk of being further distanced from decisions on monetary policy. Since, even under a regime of central bank independence, the chancellor is bound to stay close to the governor, the Treasury remains close to the decisions (a Treasury observer attends meetings of the Monetary Policy Committee). It is far more difficult for the prime minister to retain any purchase on decisions if they are made in the Bank of England. A third argument was that it could be dangerous to hand monetary policy to the Bank out of despair at the government's inability to make appropriate decisions. So stabilization was necessary first. A final factor, which may well have weighed in the balance with Margaret Thatcher, was that central bank independence was sometimes presented as a precursor of membership of Economic and Monetary Union. It was, certainly, a necessary condition of EMU, but it also stood on its own merits as a superior means of conducting an independent monetary policy.

In retrospect, this prime ministerial opposition looks unfortunate from an economic perspective. It delayed what has evidently been a valuable reform. Also, from the perspective of the Conservative Party, the government's reluctance to free the Bank of England left a strong card in the pack for the incoming Labour government to play, one which offset Labour's traditional vulnerability to financial market pressures.

Public expenditure control

The principal mechanism through which the Treasury exerts its dominance over other parts of government is the control of public spending. All other ministries may be categorized, to a greater or lesser extent, as 'spending departments' with a natural bias towards proposing increases in their budgets, to respond to the ever growing demands of their own clients, be they schools, farmers, generals or ambassadors. As Lawson says, if the Treasury had an institutional motto, it would be 'No'. It is this dimension of the chancellor's role which makes it the loneliest job in government.

Public spending rounds are not technical accounting exercises. Their outcomes are often the clearest expression of the government's political priorities. So there is no realistic possibility of putting public spending choices on autopilot, so to speak. Yet throughout the period chancellors, and their chief secretary lieutenants, have sought means of injecting more realism and predictability into the process.

Healey's major contribution was the introduction of annual cash limits – fixed ceilings on what each department could spend in a given year. This may seem the most basic of constraints, but before the introduction of cash limits, spending rounds were carried out in what were termed 'survey prices', and then subsequently adjusted for whatever the inflation rate turned out to be. There was therefore a natural inflationary bias in the public finances, or at least embedded resistance to inflationary pressure. Departments initially resisted cash limits strongly – how could they then accommodate wage settlements which turned out higher than forecast? Yet Healey forced this new discipline through, on the back of the IMF crisis, an inheritance for which his successors have been grateful. Forward planning in cash terms followed in 1981.

Howe notes that his contribution was to require that finance should determine expenditure, and not vice versa. Again, this seems elementary. In practice, however, setting a forward path for public spending in the context of a Medium Term Financial Strategy was a significant change. It established a clear link between monetary growth, the government's own borrowing requirement, and spending. As has been noted, in practice the discipline was somewhat weakened by the erratic behaviour of the government's target aggregate, £M3, but the principle was an important one to establish. Howe notes that Gordon Brown's 'golden rule' whereby *current* spending should be in balance over the cycle owes much to this twenty-year-old framework.

Although the MTFS was an improvement on what went before, it did not remove the need for difficult decisions when economic circumstances dictated them. Lawson asserts that he was the 'only chancellor since the war to have presided over a substantial reduction in public expenditure as a share of GDP' (figure 1.7). He also lifts the veil on some of the techniques now used by the Treasury to maintain discipline. No minister may put a proposal to Cabinet without a paragraph explaining the spending consequences and the Treasury's view of them.

During the Howe and Lawson years a special Cabinet committee known colloquially as the 'Star Chamber', usually chaired by the deputy prime minister, performed a mediation and arbitration function in relation to ministerial bids for more. Lamont sought to reassert top-down spending control from the Treasury and sat in the chair of the committee himself.

Here he says little on the techniques of public expenditure control, though he does note that his 1992 budget was over-expansionary, which demonstrates that any control mechanism, however well designed, may be overridden by a government with a difficult election to win.

When the consequences of the 1992 budget became clear, Clarke was obliged to pay much more attention to public spending, which was still – in spite of Howe's reforms – essentially based on an annual bidding process.

Following the Lamont reform, the chancellor, as Clarke explains, was the judge and jury in his own court. Michael Portillo, then the chief secretary, 'was a more than competent presenter of the Treasury's case and my adjudications in his favour were particularly easy to give.' This is another example of the Treasury tightening its grip over other departments.

Gordon Brown, after 1997, was committed to the Conservatives' spending plans for the first two years – an

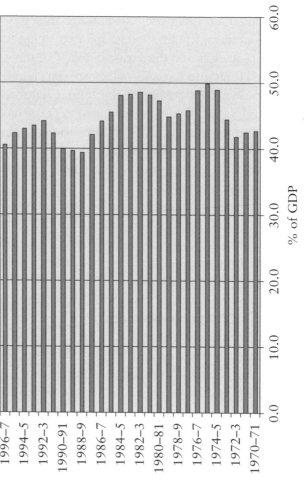

Figure 1.7   *UK government expenditure, 1970–97 (% GDP)*
Source: Her Majesty's Treasury.

unusual example of cross-party consensus, though driven by Labour's desire to build a reputation for prudence (which for a time became Brown's favourite word). More important, in the long run, was the introduction both of the golden rule and of three-year spending settlements with departments, and the abandonment of the annual bidding round.

These twin innovations seem to promise even tighter discipline on the public finances. Yet the golden rule in practice depends on judgements about the beginning and end of the economic cycle, judgements which have been exercised with the effect of allowing greater borrowing headroom. The initial rigour of the rule has been watered down significantly. And three-year plans do not preclude major upward shifts in the spending plans of particular departments, as is demonstrated by the very large planned increases in spending on health and education from 2001 onwards.

So after a period in which public spending as a proportion of GDP had stabilized, and even fallen back a little, by 2005 it was again on a rising trend. The sustainability of those increases was the biggest point of controversy about the government's economic policy as Labour moved into its third term.

Europe

Throughout the period covered by these essays Economic and Monetary Union (EMU) has been the 'ghost at the feast' of British monetary policy. The first coherent plan to create a single currency in Europe appeared in the Werner report in 1970. Healey does not refer to Werner in his contribution, which accurately reflects the lack of notice paid to it in London at the time.

EMU has, evidently, always been both a political and an economic project. It was economic, in that the dominant view in the finance ministries and central banks of Continental Europe came to be that small open economies found it increasingly difficult to maintain independent monetary policies, and needed an external anchor to help provide price stability. Furthermore, they believed that a single market would work more effectively with a single currency. It was also political, in that the pooling of economic sovereignty implied by EMU clearly points towards greater co-ordination of other policies, if not to a full political union.

It was to be twenty-nine years before the Werner proposals were consummated, but in the interim a number of attempts were made to reduce exchange rate volatility through exchange rate arrangements of different kinds, culminating in the ERM, seen explicitly as a precursor to full EMU. The UK remained outside these arrangements until the end of 1990. Margaret Thatcher was notoriously antipathetic to exchange rate manipulation – 'you can't buck the market' – but, formally, the government's policy was that it would consider joining 'when the time was ripe'. In the event, and with fateful consequences, John Major determined that ripeness had been achieved in October 1990. The sad story of Britain's short membership of the mechanism is told by Norman Lamont. Since September 1992 the UK has sat on the sidelines, while twelve countries have adopted the euro, with more of the newer EU members on the way towards EMU membership.

What do the chancellors think should now be done? Should Britain eventually exchange the euro for sterling? Here, uncharacteristically, there are significant differences of view.

Healey, while declaring himself a European, is firmly against. There can be no single currency, he believes, without a single fiscal policy, which, in turn, leads to the type of political federation he does not wish to see. He thinks, in any event, that no prospective UK government is likely to seek membership of EMU, and that 'the issue is going to sink into the sand.'

Howe does not address the euro question so directly here, but we know that he is predisposed to favour a single currency in due course, if the conditions are appropriate. His erstwhile lieutenant, Nigel Lawson, by contrast, nails his colours firmly to the 'no' mast. For Lawson, the question is 'whether it is in our national interest to pay an economic price of uncertain magnitude, coupled with the political price of giving up a major element of self-government, in return for the undefined political benefit of being "at the heart of Europe".' For him, the answer is clear: 'it cannot be.'

Lamont is equally sure of his view. While he acknowledges that ERM membership did play a useful part in shifting the UK to a new, lower, inflation path, he does not see it, and says he never saw it, as a route to the euro, to which he is firmly opposed.

Clarke, by contrast, accepts the argument that a single

market will work much better with a single currency, is unworried by the 'federalism' argument, and thinks that the UK will 'one day' adopt the euro. (In the Conservative leadership election campaign of 2005 he sought to hit the euro into the long grass, but without quite abandoning it as a desirable long-term objective.)

So we have a split vote – 3:2 – and, for now, the noes have it. All implicitly acknowledge that Bank of England independence, and the enhanced credibility that this has brought to domestic monetary policy, removes one powerful argument in favour. It cannot now be said that the UK needs to join EMU to achieve monetary stability. Was that Gordon Brown's intention in 1997, when he liberated the Bank of England, and if so did Tony Blair understand the implications of the policy he supported? Blair continued to assure other European leaders that he would engineer British membership one day, long after that seemed inconceivable. And, in any event, he had conceded policy leadership of the subject to Brown, by acquiescing in the 'five tests' plan communicated in 1998. In his book *Brown's Britain*, Robert Peston[7] describes the lengths to which Blair went in an attempt to influence the assessment of performance against the tests in 2003, without success.

For the moment, these questions are unanswerable. What is clear is that low inflation has removed some of the urgency once attached to exchange rate policy, and the commitment to a referendum (agreement to which Clarke describes as his greatest political error) makes it highly unlikely that the UK could in practice join EMU, even if the government wanted to do so.

So for the Bank of England, now entrusted with the

major policy problems confronted by the five chancellors, the stakes are high. If the Bank were to lose control of inflation and damage the credibility of the domestic inflation target regime, it is not clear what alternative is available to the government. Once again, as with ERM membership, there is no Plan B. Fortunately, at present, there is every sign that the Bank of England is up to the job.

Notes

1   I am grateful to Paolo Dasgupta, a doctoral student at the LSE, for his assistance.
2   Samuel Brittan, *Steering the Economy: The Role of the Treasury*. Harmondsworth: Penguin, 1971.
3   *The Right Approach to the Economy*. London: Conservative Central Office, 1977.
4   Letter from Norman Lamont, chancellor of the Exchequer, to John Watts MP, 8 October 1992.
5   John Maynard Keynes, *The General Theory of Employment, Interest and Money*. London: Macmillan, 1949, p. 383.
6   Derek Scott, *Off Whitehall: A View from Downing Street by Tony Blair's Adviser*. London: I. B. Tauris, 2004.
7   Robert Peston, *Brown's Britain*. London: Short Books, 2005.

2

Why the Treasury is so Difficult

Lord Healey of Riddlesden

My time in the Treasury was a difficult time in many ways. I spent six years as head of the Defence Ministry, from 1964 to 1970, and found that enormously enjoyable. I travelled all over the world, from Japan to Hawaii and to Africa, Asia and so on. I liked the people I met and went to places I could never have gone to under other circumstances, like the jungles of Borneo and the deserts of Saudi Arabia.

It was very different, yet in many ways very similar, when I went to the Treasury. It was different because there was less travel, and when I did travel it was mainly to meetings of the IMF in Europe or the United States. The only interesting place I ever went to, which I otherwise would not have visited, was Mexico, where we had one meeting which was enormous fun. I was interested to find that the Bank of Mexico had to use aircraft to move its gold around the country because if it tried to send it by road it would certainly be captured by bandits.

Yet it was similar in some ways because, when at Defence, I had, besides the Central Department, three services, the Army, Navy and Air Force, and it was rather the same at the Treasury because, besides my own department, I had to deal with the Bank of England, the Inland Revenue and the Customs and Excise, which were for practical purposes independent. The people I met were not on the whole as interesting and attractive as the people I met when I was at Defence, but some of them became friends for life – like Gordon Richardson, who was Governor of the Bank of England in my time, and Nick Monck, who was my private secretary.

In the Ministry of Defence any decision you took was implemented by people you controlled wherever they were, even if they were in Borneo or Aden. In the Treasury, the decisions you take are implemented by people over whom you have absolutely no control: employers and workers all over the country, and of course consumers, not only all over your own country but all over the world – people to whom Britain was exporting or from whom she was importing. So the control of the situation in the Treasury was infinitely more difficult than it was in Defence. On the whole I liked the people I worked with. But some of them were a little bit – 'grey', I suppose is the word. There was one official of whom it was said that he never saw a joke except by appointment.

The Bank of England was in terrible trouble when I took over because we had had the explosion of credit in 1974 and the crisis of the secondary banking system. The Bank had the very difficult job of trying to protect the value of sterling simply by raising or lowering interest rates. Its role was often described as being to exude confidence without actually lying, and to take away the punch bowl just as the party was getting merry. So it was not really a very enjoyable job to have, but Gordon Richardson, who took over at just about the same time that I took over the Treasury, was an extraordinarily able and attractive man. To look at him, very smart with fair hair, you would think he was a public schoolboy, but in fact he came from Nottingham High School, like almost everybody who was any good in my time. Douglas Wass (Permanent Secretary to the Treasury, 1974–83) came from Nottingham High School and so of course in recent times did Ken Clarke.

Gordon himself was an intelligent man with wide interests outside banking and the economy. Our relationship was one of what I would describe as creative tension, which I think is the best one can have between a chancellor and a governor. The governor's job is narrower than the chancellor's, but he has got to understand all the problems you have to deal with as well as you understand them, and you have to try to understand his problems as well as he does. He also had some very good deputies. One was a rather forbidding man called Jasper Hollom. When I asked him whether it would be wise for me to introduce monetary targets, he replied, 'Well, you would be simply redesigning your cross.' Of course he was absolutely right in that. The other deputy I saw a great deal of was Kit McMahon, who was an extremely attractive man with great interests outside economics and banking, and like me he had a passion for good American thrillers, the Black Mask type. Every time he came back from a visit to the United States he used to bring me the latest novel of George V. Higgins. Kit left the Bank of England because Maggie wouldn't appoint him as governor, so he went to the Midland Bank and saved it from disaster. It was on the point of collapse when he took it over.

The real problem, I discovered, was economics. I didn't study economics at Oxford, but I discovered very, very soon that economics is not a science, it is a branch of social psychology. People try to make generalizations from situations described by their teachers when they were students which had actually occurred twenty years earlier. So economic theory tended to be based far too much on what had happened two generations earlier.

Keynes described economics very well when he said, in 1936, something like: 'practical men who believe themselves to be quite exempt from any intellectual influences are usually the slaves of some defunct economist.'[1] I fear this may still be true; it was certainly the case in my time.

What really changed everything was that Keynes had one great weakness. In his books he shows really no sense of the importance of social organizations, especially of course of the trade union movement, which could decide how the money you released in taxation was spent and how much you had to release to spend. He had no sense in his books of the importance of world trade and the way the outside world could influence your economy. In my time exports were just over 16 per cent of our Gross Domestic Product, but one day's difference in the payments for exports made a difference of £250 million in currency flows. Everything got infinitely worse just as

I took over because of the enormous increase in oil prices brought about by OPEC, which added £2.5 billion to our current account deficit and cut our GDP by 5 per cent. So I realized that it was vital to try to make ourselves less dependent on foreign oil, which meant of course investing money in our own oil in the North Sea. Unfortunately we didn't gain much from it at the time, though when Maggie Thatcher took over, North Sea oil brought an extra 5 per cent to our GDP.

The other great problem I found with economics, and indeed with the Treasury, is that inevitably you have to rely on figures when you decide what to do, but the statistics are always unreliable. I learnt this when I was in the army, because I ruptured myself on my field training course and was sent to Woolwich Barracks and then posted to replace a drunken bombardier as a railway checker on Swindon station.

I had a job of absolutely vital importance to the war effort. I had to count the number of service men and women getting off every train, getting on every train and, for some reason I still don't understand, getting off and on again, to have a drink in the bar. Of course I made up the number of those getting off and on; there was no way of checking them. I made up the number of those getting on because it was impossible on six platforms in the blackout to count them all, and I used to get the number of those getting off from the ticket collector because he used to get their tickets, and after three weeks I discovered he made up his numbers too. So I have always had a justified suspicion of statistics – and by God those suspicions were justified when I was chancellor.

Why the Treasury is so Difficult

In my first year, 1974–5, the public sector borrowing requirement – the gap between what you were actually getting in taxes and what you spent – the estimate was £4 billion too low, which in those days was 5.4 per cent of our GDP. The next year, in 1976, it was £2 billion too high, and in 1977 it was in balance, though of course I had no idea in advance that it would be. If I had known, I would never have had to have gone to the IMF for credit, which was the most difficult decision I made in my life, and also the most difficult decision I had to get through Cabinet. It was very, very difficult indeed, yet in fact totally unnecessary.

I summed up my misgivings about economic forecasts in my November statement in 1976. I said that, like long-term weather forecasts, economic forecasts are better than nothing, but their origin lies in extrapolation from a partially known past through an unknown present to an unknowable future, according to theories about the causal relationships between certain economic variables which are hotly disputed by academic economists and may in fact change from country to country or from decade to decade. So it was very, very difficult indeed. People started giving up Keynesianism because of its obvious weaknesses, and they turned instead to monetarism.

Milton Friedman, who was the most important single figure in the influence of monetarism, thought that if you could control the money supply you could control anything, but the trouble is that it is very, very difficult indeed to control the money supply. You cannot do it simply through interest rates or by the amount of money you print yourself, because people nowadays get money all the time from all over the world, and I found that even defining it was very difficult indeed. An example of that is Arthur Burns, who was the chairman of the US Federal Reserve Bank. He told Congress, 'Let me go to the month of February. We published a figure of 6.5 per cent for the growth of money supply. If we had been using a different seasonal adjustment it might have been 10.6 per cent, and that's not the end of the story, as these figures are often revised.' This is still the great problem, defining and measuring money, and why using money supply as the key to controlling the economy is a waste of time. I always think President Johnson was right. When Ken Galbraith, the great Canadian economist, went into the Oval Office and started telling Johnson what he thought about the American economy, Johnson put his great paw on Ken's thigh and said, 'Did you ever think, Ken, that making a speech on economics is a lot like pissing down your leg? It may seem hot to you, but it never does to any one else.' Of course that is all too true.

The best judgement on economics was made by a certain Richard, the son of Nigel – not Nigel Lawson, by the way, because this was around about AD 1170. He was Treasurer of England and at the same time Bishop of London, because God and Mammon were not quite so separate in those days as they are supposed to be today. He wrote in Latin, but I'll translate it: 'The highest skill of the Exchequer does not lie in calculations but in judgement of all kinds.' That is absolutely true. The problem is judgement, and to make good judgements you have to be bright, but you also have to have a great deal of experience and to learn a lot from the experience of others. You must also recognize that the economic situation changes from country to country, from year to year, and so the rules on which you make judgements are very rarely reliable.

Almost every night when I was chancellor I wrote in my diary: 'Went to bed dog tired'. It was very, very tiring indeed, and of course became increasingly so as information technology began to take over. So you could be woken up at four in the morning by some news which had just arrived from Tokyo or Washington. My health got worse and worse when I was chancellor. I even got a bad attack of shingles because of my exhaustion. In some ways I think the British Treasury in those days was the most difficult one in the world because it tried to deal simultaneously with both finance and the economy, and in most of the countries which compete with us there were separate departments dealing with money and the economy.

But we had one advantage which many countries do not have, in that I could almost certainly rely, although it was difficult occasionally, on getting my decisions through parliament, whereas in the United States, as you know, no president or treasury secretary can ever rely on getting a decision adopted by the Congress. Very often the two houses of Congress, the Senate and the House of Representatives, disagree, so you get what they call gridlock. So we had some advantages and some disadvantages.

I was also very lucky because I had very good people working with me. Joel Barnett, who did public expenditure, was quite brilliant, very hard working, very able, and I finally managed to persuade Wilson to put him in the Cabinet so he had an independent role. Bob Sheldon was very good. Jack Diamond was brilliant. They were all from the north of England: Joel and Bob were both from Manchester, and Jack Diamond was from Yorkshire. The best of the lot was Edmund Dell, who is too often forgotten because, very soon after being there, he went to the Department of Trade and then he left politics to go and work in the City, where he really wasted the rest of his life doing nothing of much importance.

The most interesting chap I had working with me was a double agent. Harold Lever was appointed by Harold Wilson to be a spy in the Treasury, but I also used him to spy on Number 10. He was absolutely brilliant because he had an understanding of money, though not so much of the economy. If you were ever short of a million pounds, when he left the office he used to pick up the telephone and make it in a couple of calls.

The most difficult problems I had were with the unions. The trade union barons were an appalling lot in my time. They never consulted their members on what they did. Very often the union policy changed by 180 degrees when the union leader changed. The most difficult period of my life was the so-called Winter of Discontent, when we had several months of mass strikes all over the country and the economy almost came to a halt. The unions almost destroyed our motor car industry, but in the end I developed quite good relations with them. I used to have regular meetings, spent twelve hours a week as chairman of a pay committee which included

the union leaders as well as the employers and other officials from various spending departments, and in the end
I think we made quite a go of it. I persuaded Jack Jones
and Hugh Scanlon, who were called the terrible twins at
that time, to work quite well with me. I soon discovered,
incidentally, that the tradition was always to give trade
union leaders when you met them beer and sandwiches,
but I found it was better to give them a proper meal, and
I discovered before long that Hugh Scanlon's favourite
dish was *goujons de sole*. So I always arranged that we
had *goujons de sole* when I had them to discuss things
with me at Number 11.

Our pay policy in the end was quite successful. It cut
the retail price index from the appalling level of 26.9 per
cent to 19.9 per cent in 1978, and then to 4.5 per cent,
and then unfortunately it collapsed – I think because I
set the target too low. I think if, rather than going for 5
per cent, I had said single figures, we would have had settlements of about 11 per cent, whereas the settlements
they were agreeing were rising – 24 per cent in one year,
40 per cent in fact in the case of one trade union.

One of the most important changes I think in British
politics and economics was when we decided to force
union leaders to consult their members before they took
decisions. We have not really had much of a problem
since then. In fact I often envy Gordon Brown and Tony
Blair their good luck in living in a Britain where the trade
unions are not a serious problem and there is no important challenge either in policy or personality from the
left wing. There is no Tony Benn or Nye Bevan as we
used to have, so life is very much easier, and of course the

divisions inside parties these days are really deeper in the Tory Party than in the Labour Party. The nearest thing to a left-winger these days is Peter Hain.

I found in the end the only way to control public spending was to set cash limits to the amount of money that was spent by each department. Oddly enough they over-worked, because a lot of the departments actually spent a good deal less than they were given as a limit because they were terrified of going above the level set for them. As I have mentioned, our pay policy in the end cut the annual increase in the RPI from 26.9 per cent to 19.9 per cent, and we got unemployment and inflation down at the same time before long, which in those days was pretty well a record in Britain, and indeed in most countries. The key figure in making a success of all that was a friend of mine whom I had known since Oxford, who later became chairman of the Fabian Society, Leo Pliatzky. One of the tragedies of British politics was that Leo died comparatively young. I think he could have been a major influence for good on economics in our country.

I did achieve one thing, however. I cut government spending on ministers' salaries and I forced ministers to pay tax if they lived in a government home, so oddly enough, although as chancellor I was working twice as hard as I worked as defence secretary, my take-home pay was only half what I got as defence secretary. But that was my fault and I do not actually regret it.

The real problem I discovered before long in the British economy was not really government financial policy, it was the inferior management in British industry. Getting that right was appallingly difficult for a government to do. We tried to influence it through the NEDC, the National Economic Development Council, but we had only limited success. We were also, because we depended so much on foreign trade, exceptionally dependent on what was happening in the world economy. For example, the OPEC oil price increase added £2.5 billion to our current account deficit, a colossal amount, and then of course along came the information technology revolution. By 1988 fifty times more money was crossing our exchanges than the whole of our public expenditure, and the influence of information technology on our economy was the thing we found very, very difficult to control.

Fortunately in my last years I became chairman of the Interim Committee of the IMF, which was effectively the Executive Committee of the IMF, and I got to know most of my foreign colleagues very well, especially the Americans like Bill Simon, Ed Yeo and Arthur Burns and, in Europe, Raymond Barre in France and Helmut Schmidt in Germany. He became my closest friend for the rest of my life in European politics because we also had been defence secretaries before that. We had some very good people to work with. I also liked very much Jacques Delarosière in France, who was head of the IMF itself in my time. One of the most interesting things was getting to know the Japanese. I found it very difficult to speak to the Japanese if we needed a translator, because it took such a long time, but the best Japanese all spoke very good English and they were brilliant without exception.

Well, in 1976 I needed a £5.3 billion standby credit. Then I got support from the IMF on condition that I cut

£1 billion of our public spending, but the pound then went up and up, interest rates came down to 5 per cent, and yet I had used only half of the money I was offered by the IMF. I had paid it all back by the time I left the Treasury.

On the whole, although it was very tiring work, I did enjoy my time at the Treasury because in the end I managed to leave the economy in a much better state than when I inherited it from Tony Barber.

Surprisingly, I became quite a popular chancellor, and the polls showed that I had become the most popular politician in the country. I think this was all due to my eyebrows. They've always embarrassed me slightly, and once I shaved them off for that reason, but my trousers fell down so I had to let them grow again.

The tragedy is that on the whole the Treasury job was pretty successful, but of course by that time the nature of politics in Britain had changed enormously. Jim Callaghan said he thought there was a wind of change. People had got fed up with what they called the nanny state, so Maggie Thatcher won and took over, and that is another story.

Questions and Answers

I would like to ask you about the leadership contest for the Labour Party which you lost. Can you tell us what the real reasons were for your defeat? I remember in particular hearing Roy Hattersley say that there was a campaign on the part of some MPs deliberately not to vote for you in order to weaken the Labour Party and strengthen the SDP.

I think the basic reason was that I had to do so many unpopular things when I was chancellor, and it is very difficult for a chancellor to get the top job. It has only happened once or twice. It is Gordon's problem too. Also I wasn't terribly keen on being prime minister. The job I really wanted and never got was as foreign secretary. I would have loved to have had that, but for a variety of reasons I just wasn't available at the suitable time. I never really worked hard to be leader of the party and there is no question that one of the reasons was that I made so many enemies in the trade union movement, and the trade unions dominated the party in those days. And, as I say, the barons didn't really take much notice of their members. For example, when I went for the Deputy Leadership, the Transport and General Workers Union by a majority of one vote in their group at party conference voted for Benn rather than me, although I had a 95 per cent majority in a poll they'd done of their own members earlier on. But that's life, isn't it!

Could you comment on the importance of the early membership of the European Community in the 1970s and on the euro, and whether or not Britain should join.

Well, I have always been very, very keen on Britain working with the Europeans. When I was defence secretary, for example, I set up the European Planning Group inside NATO. But I have never been in favour of

European federation, which was the stated objective of the people like Jean Monnet who started the European movement. In practice, of course, support for federation in Europe is limited to the very small countries such as Holland and Luxembourg. The French would never support being members of a federation, nor in practice would the Germans, although they've often talked in favour of it.

The problem to me of the euro and the European Monetary Union is that you cannot have a single currency without having a single fiscal policy and you cannot have a single fiscal policy without having at least a federal government, and I am not in favour of that. Even now we find that the EMU is not working well, or the euro inside Europe itself. The Germans have practically now turned completely against it and the French have always really been against it, so I think in fact Gordon Brown's arguments against are totally justified – or let me say his conditions for joining, which are conditions we all know will never be met. I think we are finding as time passes that the issue is going to sink into the sand.

It is often said of Chancellor Brown that he controls a lot of the domestic agenda by virtue of the money that is allocated between departments. Was it possible for you to influence domestic policy to the same extent in your day? And, just as an aside, the story of you turning round at the airport to go back to the Labour Party conference – could you just tell us how apocryphal that is?

Well, they are two quite different questions. The first is the amount of spending allocated to departments. Well, that is decided by the Cabinet as a whole, but of course the chancellor has an enormous influence on it. I did in fact have a great deal of influence on it in my time, but not total control. In the end Barbara Castle was sacked from the Cabinet because she wouldn't go along with my policy.

The other question is a very easy one. It was the value of sterling. I was due to go to a meeting of the Commonwealth Economic Ministers in the Philippines. On the way to the airport I listened to the radio, and heard that the pound was falling very rapidly. When I got into the VIP lounge, I decided it would be a terrible mistake to be away. Jim had advised me to go to the meeting but I decided I couldn't afford to be away, especially as the party conference was taking place at that time in Scarborough. So I decided that I wouldn't go, and then I had to book an aircraft to take me from Northolt to the nearest airport to Scarborough so that I could get to the conference. Then I had to defend my policy from the floor, because I wasn't a member of the National Executive, in five minutes. When I went to the platform the whole of the enormous auditorium was booming with boos. When I sat down after saying I was going to stick to all my decisions, including the unpopular ones, I had almost as many cheers as boos, but it was one of my most difficult times.

Do you think in retrospect that Harold Wilson's creation of the Policy Unit was a useful addition and helpful to good government?

I cannot see really that it was. In principle I wouldn't be against it, but the real trouble with Harold was that he wouldn't set up any body unless he knew he controlled the majority of its members. He was quite unlike Jim Callaghan, who was prepared to take a decision against the will of the whole of the Cabinet or the Economic Committee which he had been chairing. Harold would appoint people to the Cabinet just because he knew they would do what he wanted, like Lord Chalfont. Wilson in fact was an awful prime minister; he was rather like Harold Macmillan. They were both opportunists with no real sense of values and no principles, so nothing to guide them as to what would get them through the next problem.

I was very interested in your reference to creative tension between yourself and Gordon Richardson. Could you talk for a moment about the advantages of creative tension, bearing in mind that the establishment of the Department of Economic Affairs in 1964 didn't seem to do anything very positive as a result of the creative tension between the Treasury and the DEA. Perhaps you could tell us whether you felt creative tension when Jim Callaghan told the Cabinet in the autumn of 1978 that he wouldn't go to the country?

I think between Gordon and me the creative tension was a very good thing, because we both liked and respected each other's views. Gordon, of course, had one prime responsibility which took precedence over everything else, which was the value of sterling. I was concerned with employment, equality of opportunity, all sorts of other things, so the tension between us was generally creative. I think you couldn't say that really of tension between bodies or departments. The tension there is not creative in the same sense at all. Gordon, as I say, was a very intelligent man with a lot of understanding. He had been a very successful 'merchant' banker for ten years in fact before he went to the Bank of England, and I think the relationship between the two of us was good for the economy. We remained good friends and still are now.

Should the Blair government have renationalized the railways on coming to power, and were the Labour government's policies in the 1960s and 1970s mistaken in respect of not privatizing the utilities earlier than they were under Maggie? Also, I heard you say recently that Gordon Brown is perhaps the greatest chancellor we have had. Do you really think so?

I personally think that it would have been sensible to renationalize the railways because I think that to have completely separate bodies, in different areas, is not sensible. I think the railways are in an awful mess now and perhaps renationalization would be helpful.

On the other question, I think it would have made sense to privatize some of the utilities, but frankly I don't remember enough now to know which ones. I am not against privatization in principle, but I think that privatization of the railways has been a total disaster. I don't think that's quite the same with, for example, electricity and several other areas.

As for Gordon Brown, he has been a first-rate chancellor, and our economy is doing better than any other economy in Europe at the present time. One of the most important things he's doing is stopping Tony Blair rushing into the euro. Of course he's made some mistakes. Everybody makes some mistakes, but I think he has been a very good chancellor – though he and Tony Blair have been incredibly fortunate compared with all their predecessors in that they've had no serious problems with the trade union movement and no serious challenge in policy or personality from the left.

I still have George Brown's national plans on my bookshelf. Can we ever get away from short-term horizons? Do we need an annual budget emanating from the Treasury? Do you think there can be a longer planning horizon, particularly in what is increasingly becoming a global economy?

No, I think an annual budget is quite sensible because the situation both domestically and abroad can change very, very fast. The most obvious example is the oil crisis and the possibility of the war in Iraq stopping the supply of oil from the Middle East. I think to try to plan further ahead is a mistake, but it doesn't mean that every year you have to change everything. I mean if things are going well you obviously don't want to change them.

Following on from your comments on Gordon Brown, soon after New Labour came to power in 1997 he took the important decision of handing over the setting of

interest rates to the Monetary Policy Committee of the Bank of England. How much would you say that the country's record of economic success since then has been due to that one far-sighted decision?

I think it was a sensible decision, but it is hard to say how much it has been responsible for. The really important thing with Gordon Brown is his prudence in tax and spending. That's the key, much more important than the independence of the Bank.

During your time in the Treasury you were very complimentary about many of your officials, but you found some of them to be actively disloyal and conspiring against you, didn't you? Conspiring with the Americans to force monetarism on to this country? Is that correct, and how difficult was that to deal with?

I don't recall that being the case. I obviously disagreed with some of my officials. I don't like taking decisions on the advice of the permanent secretary alone. I like to get a meeting with all the relevant people from the department, including junior people, not just heads of section, and let them argue things out in front of me, with I myself taking part as well. I think if you do it that way it works very well. It certainly did with me.

You said that combining finance and economics was not a very good idea. Certainly there is a case for there being an additional economics ministry, but how would you do it? I think you said the DEA didn't work very well.

In France and Germany they have now combined economics and finance. You were also not too impressed by the Prime Minister's Policy Unit. How actually would you set up this countervailing pole?

Also, do you think that your advisers panicked too much about sterling and perhaps did not realize sufficiently that we were on a floating rate which was bound to move up and down? Now that thirty years have passed and we are getting more of the papers, we can see many of the ridiculous emergency plans they had for a siege economy. The worst one was called Operation Brutus, which you might have inherited. Perhaps you wouldn't even have had to have turned around at London airport, even on the basis of bad figures, if you had thought of sterling as a price which goes up and down.

The first question – I much prefer the British system in which finance and the economy are under the same department, because if they are different departments you can get not a creative tension but a destructive tension between the two. I think you've got enough difference if you have an independent central bank. You don't need to have an independent finance department as well.

The other question – I agree it was a great mistake that we were too worried about sterling. The real trouble was we had too much devotion to the old systems in the financial area, I mean the opposition to ending the sterling area, for example, which was an extraordinary anomaly and had lost its ability to work once the Commonwealth countries became genuinely independent. That was a great mistake. We worried a great deal too much about our currency. That's an area where it does make sense to allow the markets to have a big influence, providing the markets are regulated.

Why is it that in America the Federal Reserve is seen as the prime mover of economic policy? For example, Arthur Burns, Paul Volcker, Alan Greenspan, what they say and what they do is more important than what the US Treasury is doing. The first time Bush became president the first person he met was Alan Greenspan. Why is it so important there, where the Federal Reserve is seen as more important than the Treasury secretary?

America is an enormous continent and requires a federal state because of the differences in the interests of different areas like the south, the west, the east, and the midwest. They have a single currency, so they need of course a single central bank, which is the Federal Reserve, and when they have good chairmen like particularly the one I knew best, Paul Volcker, I think it has worked very, very well indeed. I think Bush is taking a lot of silly decisions. I think his decision to have these big tax cuts without making it clear what spending is going to be cut at the same time is a very dangerous one.

If you were advising John Kerry today, what would you recommend him to say?

If I were advising Kerry how would I tell him he could get out of the war in Iraq? Well, the obvious thing is start negotiating with the United Nations and see if they will agree to have a protectorate in Iraq which will allow the Americans to withdraw. That is the only way of getting out now, and I think it could come to that, although it would be an awful burden on the UN of course. The American policy is an absolute disaster because it has got the whole of Iraq now turned against the United States. A civil war will follow between the Shia, the Sunni and the Kurds, and on top of that you've got a big increase in terrorism, and everybody who knows the area has been predicting this.

Would the Americans have invaded Iraq without Blair?

I don't know, but I think Blair has made several serious mistakes in his last term. The most serious by far was supporting Bush in Iraq, but equally I think he has made inexcusable mistakes on financing hospitals and university entrance fees. He's really become very like Maggie. He's like Eden on Iraq and like Maggie on poll tax and these domestic issues. I have expressed it in public, so this is a personal view but not a private one.

If James Callaghan had gone to the country in 1978 would he have won that election?

If he had gone sooner rather than hanging around for two years, I think we might have won the election. He said he stayed on to take the shine off the ball for me, but of course it ripped the leather off the ball, not just the shine. Certainly, if I had taken over from him, Maggie would have had only one term rather than thirteen years.

I think with oppositions that they tend often to go to the person who's to their ideological extreme. If the Tories had any sense they'd go now for Ken Clarke rather than Howard because they have no chance of winning under Howard. Under Ken Clarke, or even Portillo, I think they would be a serious threat to Labour. I think we made a great mistake in choosing Michael Foot. If the elections had been earlier, and won, we wouldn't have had the split with the SDP, now the Lib Dems, which took twenty-seven Labour MPs out of the house. If we had avoided that I don't think we would have had all those years of Maggie. Still, many of you would probably feel that would have been a bad thing!

Note

1   John Maynard Keynes, *The General Theory of Employment, Interest and Money*. London: Macmillan, 1949.

3

Can 364 Economists all be Wrong?

Lord Howe of Aberavon

It must be acknowledged, I hope, that of the four Cabinet posts which I have been lucky enough to hold, that of chancellor of the Exchequer is manifestly the one in which it is most difficult to be widely loved. And it is also probably the most constantly difficult. When Denis Healey rang to congratulate me on my appointment as his successor at Number 11 – and his was the very first call – his greeting said it all: 'Welcome, Geoffrey', he said, 'to the bed of nails.' And rightly so. For it was in the Treasury that I appreciated most sharply, at least at first, the forceful insight of the late Edmund Dell (Denis Healey's first Paymaster General) that: 'For anyone afraid that ignorance renders him ineligible for responsibility, politics is not the right profession.'[1] And yet, and yet . . . It was as I became more and more familiar with the task of managing the nation's economic affairs that I came increasingly to wonder whether the soundness of the judgements which I had to make was necessarily, or even at all, dependent on the breadth and quality of my economic literacy.

Can 364 Economists all be Wrong?

Hence the disrespectful tone of my chosen title. For the benefit of younger readers – remember, the first of my five budgets was introduced more than a quarter of a century ago – let me try to put that title into perspective. The 364 economists in question are those who asserted in a terse letter to *The Times* of 30 March 1981, just two weeks after my third budget statement, that: 'There is no basis in economic theory or supporting evidence for the Government's present policies.' They could hardly have stated the choice more starkly: 'The time has come', they said, 'to reject monetarist policies' – and, by necessary implication, to revert to something like the preceding policy mix. For their prescription was no more specific than 'to consider urgently which alternative offers the best hope of sustained economic recovery'.

Their timing could not have been less appropriate. For it was in that very quarter that the fall in national output came to an end. Over the next eight years, real GDP grew by an average of 3.2 per cent per annum – 'sustained economic recovery', one might say. And by the end of my last year in the Treasury (June 1983) inflation was down to 3.7 per cent – lower than at any time since 1968.

No wonder I was later to joke that an economist is a man who knows 364 ways of making love – but who doesn't know any women.

The ideological flavour of the mass letter had, however, reminded me of a powerfully expert seminar which I had addressed at our Washington embassy only six months before. J. K. Galbraith had there risen to his enormous height and ironically intoned, 'I would not at all wish to discourage the Chancellor from continuing with his monetarist experiment. I would indeed deplore it if he stopped – because Friedman would then be able to say that it would have worked if only he had given it another six months.'

The 364 letter-writers had presented the choice in similarly challenging tone. Happily, however, I have never myself been temperamentally attracted by ideological absolutism – and least of all in the field of economic policy. When I arrived at the Treasury, as Edmund Dell quite rightly pointed out, 'I did not possess the technical qualifications to choose between the different measures and the different forms of control offered to [me].'[2] But, as he was also kind enough (and shrewd enough) to add, 'probably no one had the necessary qualifications, even among those claiming to be expert in the field.'

I was able, on the other hand, to draw upon my experience of having grappled with a diversity of conflicting expert evidence during twenty years of practice at the bar. The resulting 'lawyerly scepticism', which Edmund Dell also noted,[3] was certainly not erased, I have to say, by my experience of, and insight into, the dismal science (as some optimists still describe it) over a quarter of a century of active political engagement with economic issues before I ever reached the Treasury.

My tone thus far must have sounded a shade unfriendly towards economists. Let me try to correct the balance. I certainly do not seek to prove that economists are uniquely *un*qualified to determine, or at least to influence, the shape of government economic policy. Still less would I suggest that lawyers are better qualified to do so. But I do contend, in relation to all these 'expert' matters, that there is an indispensable role which only politicians can play.

Two phrases may serve to illustrate this. First, A. J. Balfour's dictum – often echoed by Alec Douglas-Home: 'Democracy is government by explanation.' And, second, a chapter heading from a book by a distinguished civil servant, C. H. Sisson: 'The politician as intruder'.[4]

A well-governed society needs people of that disposition, whose role it is to 'intrude' among the experts (of all kinds) to evaluate their thinking and advice, to evaluate the practical implications, and, not least, to explain them to people at large, so that they may understand the consequences and, often, participate in their implementation, sometimes decisively.

Those who aspire to this role (we intruders do not always recognize ourselves at first) almost inevitably find themselves drawn, indeed driven, towards problems which require some insight into economics. Hence my own twenty-five years of 'active political engagement with economic issues', before I ever reached the Treasury.

Simply to illustrate the diversity of that engagement, I hope a brief catalogue may be forgiven:

- in 1956 and 1959, co-authorship of *Houses to Let*, making the case for abolition of rent control, and *Gwaith y Gymru*, the first ever political party attempt to spell out a long-term economic policy for Wales;
- in 1961 and 1965, two Bow Group tracts on the future of the welfare state. Thanks to the kindness of one LSE scholar, I now cherish Richard Titmuss's ferociously annotated copy of one of these. The other was hailed

by Nicholas Timmins[5] as having 'summed up much of what was to be the radical right's agenda during the 1980s';

- in 1967 (if only to give the tally some balance), chairmanship of the Ely Hospital inquiry (into the maltreatment of mental hospital inmates in Cardiff) and membership of the committee, chaired by Professor Harry Street, which largely shaped the Race Relations Act 1968; and, finally,

- from 1966 to 1972, membership of the teams responsible for the evolution (and, as Solicitor General, for enactment and initial implementation) of the Industrial Relations Act 1971 and the European Communities Act 1972.

Then came my first direct ministerial experience of expert economic advice – as a member of Ted Heath's Cabinet, during its last two critical years in office. My ministerial role was as fascinating as it was unusual. I was appointed as Britain's first Minister of Consumer Affairs [and Trade]. But from the outset the Prime Minister preferred to label me as 'Minister for Keeping Down Prices'. For such – in *his* eyes at least – I was expected to be. There was a special irony about that. For our prices and incomes freeze (to be followed by stages II and III of our prices and incomes policy) commenced on the day of my appointment to Cabinet, 6 November 1972 – without any prior consultation with me.

It was, of course, a massive U-turn – but one which took almost nobody by surprise. Pay settlement rates were soaring so fast (the miners had earlier that year secured a 27 per cent increase) that such a move had been virtually demanded at the Tory Party conference, just six weeks before. It was at least the fourth attempt of its kind since 1945; Stafford Cripps, Selwyn Lloyd and George Brown had all been this way before. Characteristically, under Ted Heath's leadership, our ill-fated attempt was more absolutist than ever before. Throughout it all, I was one of the small group of ministers (along with the PM, Chancellor and Employment Secretary) who spent almost every weekend and most days – or so it now seems – either at Chequers or at Number 10, closeted with TUC or CBI or both – or just with each other!

And on 4 March 1974 it all ended in tears. Ted Heath had tendered his resignation and Harold Wilson was back in Downing Street.

I certainly do not propose to revisit the history of the five years, about which Denis Healey has already made mention. I shall invite you instead to consider for a moment the longer period, between my first and second *arrivals* in government – first, on 18 June 1970, with Ted Heath; and later, on 3 May 1979, with Margaret Thatcher. How had our minds moved during that decade? How, at least, had my own thinking evolved? How did the events of those nine years help to shape the policies which later earned the sobriquet of Thatcherism?

Any answer to these questions must start from an understanding of the atmosphere which surrounded our arrival in office in 1979. The most important feature was indisputable. Nobody by then could any longer doubt that Britain – and above all our economy – was in deep,

deep trouble. For the second (or even a third) time in five years a government had been driven from office by industrial strife. The turmoil of the Three-Day Week had been more than matched by the Winter of Discontent. Unemployment and inflation were both frighteningly high and rising. Our relative economic decline was close to becoming absolute.

And, most important of all, this perception was becoming more and more widely and well understood at home and abroad. Sir Nicholas Henderson's [British Ambassador to France, 1975–9] well-leaked Paris dispatch brutally, and correctly, had described Britain as 'the Sick Man of Europe'. The soon-to-depart Prime Minister, James Callaghan, had shrewdly identified these truths when he told his then special adviser, Bernard Donoughue, that 'There are times, perhaps once every thirty years, when there is a change in politics . . . a shift in what the public wants . . . I suspect there is now such a sea-change.'[6]

All this was destined to give our incoming government a significant advantage. For there were, at last and at least, some spreading seeds of understanding of the need for a new beginning, with the prospect of a long haul ahead. My first budget had to (and did) signal just that, by offering a clear idea of our policy objectives and methods – and a strong political will to succeed. Margaret Thatcher's tenacity was to be crucial here, of course. We had to signal too that there was to be a substantial change in approach – to signal, if you like, that 'the US cavalry had arrived'. Hence, perhaps, the impression (which I gained on arrival at the Treasury) that the then Permanent

Secretary, Sir Douglas Wass, 'was sceptically eager, along with most of his colleagues, to join in a genuinely fresh and determined onslaught on the "British disease" with which they had grappled in vain for so long.'[7]

They were not to be disappointed by the freshness of our approach. And gradually, I believe, they came to appreciate – and to share with a wider audience – the view that few, if any, of our proposals had emerged without a good deal of thought. James Callaghan had rightly identified his thirty-year timescale for fundamental political change.

For the great majority of those who came to form the core of Margaret Thatcher's Cabinet had cut their political teeth, as I had done, in the general elections of 1950 and 1951, which signalled the end of the Attlee revolution. The next two decades witnessed the acceptance of many of the virtues of that period. However, beneath the apparent consensus of 'Butskellism', from which the Wilson governments had not dramatically departed, people were beginning to perceive its neglected or developing defects. Hence – at the risk of most unseemly vanity and simply as an example of many others – my own 1960s essay, which Nicholas Timmins noticed as having identified the radical right's agenda for the 1980s.

Hence too, and of far greater significance, the whole tone and content of the Heath manifesto for the 1970 election. 'Selsdon man' (the notional author of that document) did indeed blaze a trail that was eventually to play a part in shaping the last quarter of the twentieth century – but not, alas, in the Heath decade itself. Yet those were the years which started to define many of the crucial changes that were to come. And I was lucky enough to be amongst those who were either in the front row of the stalls or on stage throughout that formative period.

I believe that our most fundamentally important perceptions were fourfold.

First and foremost came the (eventually overriding) realization that inflation, on anything like the scale that was becoming endemic, was entirely incompatible with the creation or preservation of a stable, fair and efficient society. It was indeed hard for those of us whose childhood and early adult world had been one of virtually stable prices to abandon that premise. Hence the determination of successive governments to give priority to this objective.

Second – not perhaps in prominence but in our readiness to admit – was the perception that economic flexibility and efficiency, indeed success of any kind, were being stifled by over-regulation (and all too often by the consequences of public ownership). Harold Wilson's 'bonfire of controls' (when he was at the Board of Trade in the Attlee government) was only the first of many indecisive infernos of that kind. The whole apparatus of price, income, dividend and exchange control was to become the most intrusive example of continuing failure on this front.

Third was the long-neglected need for dramatic change in the structure of our tax system – above all for a decisive switch from direct to indirect taxation. It is almost impossible now to recall – even to believe – the penal top income tax rates of that era – higher than anywhere else in the world, except Albania. Change on this front was to be one of the most explicit features of my first budget.

Finally, and most important, was the eventual acceptance of the case for far-reaching reforms of the labour market. It had taken decades for this view to prevail – not least because the 'Giant's Strength'[8] of trade union bargaining power had not been fully realized or exploited until some years after it had been refurbished by the Trade Disputes Act of 1946. The impact of this imbalance was significantly increased, moreover, in cases where a monopoly union found itself engaged in what was often a potentially malign partnership with a state-owned monopoly employer. This was much more often the case than it once had been, as a result of the nationalization programme of the Attlee government.

Remarkably, but not perhaps surprisingly, this issue had only become admissible to serious political debate during the first Wilson government. Lord Donovan's Royal Commission on this subject was appointed in April 1965. The 'Battle of Downing Street' described in Peter Jenkins's book of that name[9] took place only after the Prime Minister had called in vain upon AEU General Secretary 'Hughie' Scanlon to 'take your tanks off my lawn!'. Then came Barbara Castle's courageous 1968 White Paper 'In Place of Strife', which foreshadowed many of the provisions of our 1971 Industrial Relations Act. These were, in large part, repealed by Michael Foot in 1974. (I say 'in large part' because one of the most important features of that Act survives – and most fruitfully so – to this day. I have in mind the Employment Appeal Tribunal, whose existence and shape springs in detail from the 1971 Act: in all but name it is the originally much-hated National Industrial Relations Court.) By 1979, therefore, the crying need for reform of the labour market was certainly an idea whose time had come. The 1978–9 Winter of Discontent had made certain of that.

These four topics dominated the agenda for the whole of my four years as Shadow Chancellor, from 1975 to 1979. It was, moreover, an agenda which we had good reason to believe we should soon be called upon to implement. Labour had come to office with an overall majority of only four, soon whittled away by by-election defeats. So they became politically dependent on their pact with the Liberal Party and economically dependent, after the sterling crisis of 1976, on the policy-makers of the International Monetary Fund. It was at that year's Labour Party conference that James Callaghan bluntly dismissed the notion of increasing employment by 'spending your way out of a recession'. It was, he said: 'an option that no longer exists . . . and, insofar as it ever did exist, only worked on each occasion by injecting bigger doses of inflation into the economy, followed by higher levels of unemployment as the next step.' Those words of wisdom have often been attributed to Peter Jay – but they were spoken by the Prime Minister.

For the remainder of its time in office, the Labour government was committed to the achievement of quantified monetary targets. It cannot, therefore, be too often stated that, by the time the Thatcher government came into office, this was already an established part of British economic policy. Labour had made a virtue out of IMF necessity, and we went on to make a necessity out of Labour's reluctant virtue.

That was the background to the work which I chaired in the party's Economic Reconstruction Group and which led to the production in October 1977 of the 54-page policy document *The Right Approach to the Economy*.[10] This had been co-authored, hammered out indeed, by Keith Joseph, Jim Prior, David Howell and myself – and edited by Angus Maude. I had taken pains to ensure the exclusion from our thinking of what I called 'theological absolutes'. No 'incomes policy' but certainly a 'policy for incomes', clearly related to targeted reduction of monetary growth. This would need to be discussed with major participants in the economy, probably best in the National Economic Development Council (NEDC), which still existed. We also proposed (and in office secured) a number of moves towards a more independent role for the Bank of England: the governor became, most valuably, a member of the NEDC, or Neddie, as we knew it, and was in regular public contact with the Treasury and Civil Service Select Committee – only one of a number of such bodies that came into existence after our election in 1979. It was the beginning of a process which was eventually to take decisions about interest rates out of Number 10 Downing Street, via 'the Ken and Eddie show', to the Monetary Policy Committee.

Our most anxious discussions concerned the search for an enduring way out of formal incomes policy. One or two 'theologians' confidently argued that all would fall into place in response to clearly managed monetary restraint. I had no such belief in automaticity. We had to persuade actors in the labour market that it was for them to understand and respect the constraints on their bargaining position. Repeatedly, I stressed our commitment not to 'free' (which implied 'reckless') collective bargaining but to 'responsible collective bargaining, free from government interference'. It was this which we were eventually able to achieve. Probably the largest obstacle to that conclusion was our Shadow Cabinet's pre-election decision – against my strong advice and Margaret's slightly less robust instinct – to honour the recommendations of the so-called Clegg Commission on public sector pay, which had just been set up by our Labour predecessors.

Alongside this process of policy formulation, we had, of course, to address the problems of persuading the electorate – both before and after the election of 3 May 1979. By good fortune we had available – at least to the inner Shadow Cabinet – one resource, whose existence has been little noticed but whose thinking was of long-term significance. I have in mind the so-called Stepping Stones project, which was led by John Hoskyns, a successful IT entrepreneur, who was now restless to play a part in tackling Britain's economic mess – and had the resources (and the independence) that would allow him to do so. The story of Stepping Stones is very fully described in Hoskyns's own memoir.[11]

He had in fact tried to sell his thinking within other political parties – and eventually found an eager taker in Keith Joseph. Hoskyns, once blessed by Margaret Thatcher, had joint overseers in Keith and myself. His first report reached our desks in November 1977. To a large extent it was a fortification of thoughts, which some of us had been developing since the 1960s. Its special value was to put these into a deeper and longer perspective. The central thesis was that the necessary sea-change in Britain's political economy would require much more than a Tory landslide to carry them through. Our strategy had to include long-term plans for the avoidance or removal of political obstacles to its implementation. The greatest of these was, of course, the negative stance of the trade unions. To compete with Labour in seeking co-existence with an *unchanged* union movement would ensure continued economic decline, however much masked initially by North Sea oil. Skilfully handled, however, the rising tide of public feeling could transform the unions from the Labour Party's secret weapon into its major liability. This way the fear – on our own part, as much as anybody else's – of union – Tory conflict could be laid to rest.

This essential insight was powerfully validated by experience during the 1978–9 Winter of Discontent. Equally crucial to our whole approach was the perception that there were plenty of other things that needed to be put right – in management, in education, in government, across the board. Most important was the recognition that, for all its fundamental significance, this was a strategy that certainly should not be launched in any kind of blitzkrieg – but had to be followed discreetly and unfolded gradually, step by step.

In this context, Margaret Thatcher's initial enthusiasm was, to the surprise of some, sensibly tempered by her instinct for caution. This was reflected in the tone of our 1979 manifesto. Our collective judgement was thereafter shaped by an uneasy, but mercifully developing, balance – between radicals like Margaret, Keith, myself and Norman Tebbit (an unusual alliance) and, on the other hand, people such as Willie Whitelaw, Quintin Hogg and Jim Prior. Events conspired to bring hearts and heads together. The basic analysis was thus able to offer guidance for years ahead – as reckless union leadership continued to make our case, at least until the conclusion of the miners' strike of 1984–5.

But I have raced ahead of myself. Let me come back to the prospect facing us on 3 May 1979. It was clear already that the budget, which I had to present within weeks – actually on 12 June – would largely shape the nation's expectations for the years ahead. I was able to sound at least three clear notes.

First, the end of pay, price and dividend control – to a large extent the funeral of a regime that had already collapsed.

Second, the most heralded signal of all, a dramatic shift in the shape (rather than a cut in size) of the tax burden. I replaced two rates of Value Added Tax of 8 and 12.5 per cent with a single rate of 15 per cent – and thus made room for matching cuts in income tax rates. The basic rate came down from 33 to 30 per cent. Top rates of 98 and 83 per cent (on investment and earned income respectively) were slashed – by 23 per cent, to 75 and 60 per cent – and thus brought into line with the European average. These cuts in the higher rates resulted in an increased contribution from high income earners. Taken together, these changes matched the most applauded line in almost every speech I had made over the four preceding years: 'Pay as You Spend makes far more sense than Pay as You Earn'.

The third signal was our determination to rein back the ongoing growth in public borrowing and expenditure. Denis Healey's exploitation of what he called 'sod off year' (his escape from IMF surveillance, during 1978–9) inevitably overcame Joel Barnett's gallant struggle to restrain this recidivist slippage. By contrast, I made it very clear that 'finance must determine expenditure and not expenditure finance'. This objective was, unsurprisingly, set within the context of continuing the monetary framework of counter-inflationary discipline, which had been adopted by Denis Healey, at the behest of the IMF, in September 1976.

Remarkably, one or two ministerial colleagues retrospectively claimed to be 'shocked' by this presentation. Other observers were more accurate. 'It's what you voted for', proclaimed *The Economist*'s front cover – echoed even by the *Daily Mirror*: 'No one who voted Conservative can complain.'

All this was, of course, only the first step in a continuing programme of structural change, which had been far too long postponed. The difficulties resulting from this national procrastination were inevitably increased, as we were soon to be reminded, by the fact that this programme was being undertaken at a time of global economic turmoil. But the timing was not of our choosing. There was nothing to be gained by delay.

The next highly visible step along the way was my announcement, on 23 October 1979, of the abolition of exchange control. This had been stifling financial markets and distorting investment choices for forty years. My announcement was greeted by many with disbelief. Denis Healey denounced it as 'reckless and doctrinaire'; Enoch Powell envied me 'the opportunity and the privilege' of announcing a step that would 'strengthen our economy and help restore our national pride'.

William Keegan predicted, predictably, the early reintroduction of controls 'in the absence of economic miracles'. He is still waiting. As has proved to be the case with almost all the strategic decisions that we were to take, such policy reversals were never to be made. Michael White's comment in *The Guardian* was more personal: 'Sir Geoffrey has come of age. After years in the shadow of Ted and then Margaret, he must now be considered a menace in his own right.'

The rest of my time at the Treasury was never to be anything but a roller-coaster ride. Just a week later my Chief Secretary, John Biffen, had to announce our first major public spending review – that next year's total (1980–81) would be no higher than in the current year. This meant pruning our predecessors' plans by £3500 million (in today's figures, about £9 billion).

Less than two weeks later came the first of many blows of a different kind: our first major funding crisis. In retrospect it has become clearer to me than it was at the time that these were to do more to influence our week-to-week decision-taking, and even our strategic thinking, than almost any theoretical analysis. This particular crisis was triggered by publication of the money-supply figures for October – sterling M3 was growing at an annual rate of 14 per cent, well outside our target range of 7 to 11 per cent. Much more important, in practical terms, than the figure itself was the consequential fact that the purchasers of government debt were flatly unwilling to finance our borrowing at the then minimum lending rate of 14 per cent. But this was not seen as astonishing, since inflation was running at an annual rate of 16 per cent. So it was in the United States, where interest rates had recently risen as high as 18 per cent.

These were the circumstances in which we had above all to answer the question: whence, how and at what price were we to raise the money that we needed? Over succeeding months and years, this question recurred time and again. It was bound to do so, until we had secured effective control of our borrowing (and, to that end, of expenditure) and of inflation – and thus, if we achieved success on both those fronts, of monetary growth and of interest rates.

In response to my first such crisis, I had no option but to announce an 'austerity package' – in this case an accelerated payment of North Sea oil taxes and a 3 per cent hike in interest rates, to the then unprecedented level of 17 per cent. This was a dramatic illustration of the switch-back which had characterized Britain's economic management for years – and still threatened to do so. It was driving us to examine and re-examine many features – two in particular at this time. The first involved reappraisal of every possible way of measuring and, above all, controlling monetary growth, including (in the end, twice over) monetary base control (MBC). The Prime Minister was recurrently fascinated by this – in

Nigel Lawson's time as well as mine – because it looked as though it had a magic potential for delivering lower inflation without requiring higher interest rates. In the result, MBC has never been adopted in any major economy as the foundation of monetary policy.

In truth, at a time of such economic volatility it was to prove practically impossible to establish any single monetary indicator as consistently the 'right' one.[12] In 1972–4, when I was defending the Heath government's economic policy, it was very late in the day before I was briefed even to mention such a thing. Eventually, however, in answer to critics who pointed to the alarming growth of £M3 (from 10.4 to 28.1 per cent between 1970–71 and 1972–3), I was then counselled by the Treasury to focus on £M1, whose growth rate had *fallen*, over the same period, from 16.5 to 7.8 per cent.

Ten years later, however, during my time as chancellor, the monetary roles had ironically been reversed: by then we were praying in aid the broader aggregates, notably sterling M3 (which had the intellectual – and political – advantage of continuity with the IMF/Healey era), while our critics were by then citing the narrower bases, £M0 or £M1. No wonder we had our difficulties.

But one feature, to me at least, remained clear – and that was the essentially market-based link between the scale of our prospective borrowing and the price we had to pay for it, and the corresponding link between those figures and the resulting rate of inflation. Even if there was no agreement as to exactly how it should be measured, excessive monetary growth appeared to be (indeed, was) an inevitable component of these conditions.

Can 364 Economists all be Wrong?

This was the basis upon which there had evolved – with invaluable input from Nigel Lawson (and Terry Burns, whom I had appointed Chief Economic Adviser, at the age of thirty-five, soon after my arrival at the Treasury) – the Medium Term Financial Strategy. This was a central feature of my second (1980) budget speech, in which we set out a four-year path for monetary growth, public spending and tax policies. By 1983–4 (the last year covered by our plans) the target rate of monetary growth was to be halved, to about 6 per cent. The case for such an approach struck me then, as it does now, as common sense rather than revolutionary. It was a natural follow-through from the sensible IMF lesson that had been absorbed by our predecessors. And I have to say that it does not strike me as essentially different from the framework of 'golden rules' with which today's Chancellor has sought to maintain economic self-discipline and his reputation for 'prudence'.

And it was this framework of discipline which largely determined the shape of my next (1981) budget – the one which attracted the wrath of the eponymous economists who inspired the title of this chapter. It was a budget whose formulation attracted a welter of conflicting expert advice, starting with deep disagreement about monetary policy.

On the one hand, we were seriously overshooting our current monetary targets – which we were being pressed to abandon, in favour of less severe alternatives. On the other hand, and whatever the answer to the monetary dispute, we all wanted to get interest rates down – for its own sake and because the pound was, by any practical standards, too high. If that was to happen, we had to borrow less.

Not one of my advisers thought we could let the 1981–2 public sector borrowing requirement (PSBR) go hang. Absent any change in the tax burden, the out-turn was forecast at 6 per cent of GDP. If we were to have any chance of getting back on track – for inflation, as well as for interest rates – that had to come down at least to 4 per cent of GDP. The Prime Minister's advisers – but not the Prime Minister herself – had wanted me to go further than that.

My final decision was to raise taxes by £4 billion (double indexation of all excise duties, freezing of all income tax thresholds and increased oil taxation). This at least enabled me – or so we then thought – to secure a 2 per cent reduction of MLR, to 12 per cent, while still keeping us more or less on track for the sharply reduced inflation rate of 3.7 per cent, which Nigel Lawson was eventually to inherit from me.

It was the scale – indeed, the very fact – of this tax increase which was the prime affront to the collective wisdom of the 364. Yet in the result it less than completely served its one essential purpose, of enabling us to manage the government's debt in the months ahead. That became apparent from the behaviour of the exchange rate, and of markets more generally. By mid-August the pound, $2.37 at the start of the year, had fallen to a four-year low of $1.75. A month later, on the advice of Gordon Richardson, governor of the Bank, and fearful of our ability to fund the PSBR, I had to reverse the 2 per cent cut in MLR (which had been almost the only cheerful feature of the 1981 budget). And two weeks later, on the eve of the Conservative Party conference, I had to do the same again.

If we had aimed, in my controversial 1981 budget, for a smaller PSBR, I might well have got away with the original cut. As it was, the 16 per cent rate served to restore confidence, and within a few months it proved possible to bring the base rate down again. I may be forgiven, I hope, if I quote here again from Edmund Dell: 'There was little evidence that, until the 16 per cent MLR, Howe's political courage in raising taxes in a recession had sufficiently impressed the market. In his budget, he had moved in the right direction, but not far enough.'[13] That is a verdict which will certainly surprise some of you. But you will be relieved to hear that it is where I intend to end this round-by-round review.

When I left the Treasury two years later, the economy was, as I have said, well into its longest period of growth for many years, with inflation at its lowest since 1968. But unemployment was over 3 million, still rising – and, it must be said, inevitable. For I am as certain now as I was then that it was absolutely vital in 1979–81 to direct policy to defeating inflation. The price was high and deeply regrettable, but inescapable. There was bound to be a cost in slow, even negative, growth. I had seen, for example, the fall in numbers employed at the Abbey Steelworks in my home town, Port Talbot, from almost 12,000 to under 5000 – but with the plant still able to produce at least the same amount of steel.

That such changes had to be experienced to deal with inflation was a tragedy that did indeed have its roots in the past. But it was only by our willingness, our determination indeed, to make and accept such changes – almost throughout the economy – that Britain was able, slowly but eventually, to achieve by 1986 the lowest unemployment rate in Europe.

For the last time, let me quote again from Edmund Dell, this time about the 1981 budget itself: 'There is no evidence', he wrote, 'that a wiser chancellor could have more sensitively modulated the severity of his action if he was serious in his attack on inflation'; and, in a wider context just a few pages later: 'No previous post-war chancellor had bequeathed to his successor so few problems that would cause anxiety in the market place.'

To put all this, finally, into a less personal context (though I know you will not wish to blame me for taking this opportunity for self-defence), a more comprehensive judgement from another commentator, who was never perceived as a friend of the Conservative Party, the late Peter Jenkins. He was writing on the tenth anniversary of Margaret Thatcher's arrival in Downing Street (words which I quoted when proposing her health at a celebratory dinner on the same day): 'History will surely recognise her achievements as Britain's first woman Prime Minister, a leader with the courage of her convictions, who assailed the conventional wisdom of the day, challenged and overthrew the existing order, changed the political map, and put her country on its feet again.'[14]

Can 364 Economists all be Wrong?

Questions and Answers

From the perspective of a chancellor, what is your assessment of the role of economic advisers and the Policy Unit at Number 10 Downing Street? Was it a help to you, or a hindrance?

I think that the existence of any partly independent source of advice at Number 10, whether it is on economic policy or foreign policy, is bound to make government more difficult, although if it is properly used, which requires perhaps more patience than is often available, it can improve the quality of government. I think, for example, when we were having our disputes about ways of managing monetary growth, there was a huge, Alan Walters-led, critique taking place there, which had been troublesome (although not in any unhappy way).

On the other hand, when the time came to shape the 1981 budget, the arguments between Number 10 and ourselves at expert level were carried to a conclusion which we all at the end thought was about right. I became determined, once I knew of the importance of the Number 10 Economic Unit, to be sure we were alongside it. Peter Middleton went to all the Alan Walters meetings, Alan Walters went to all the Peter Middleton meetings. It didn't continue like that. If I may give an example. It was at the time when I was foreign secretary and we were considering our approach to the Madrid Summit, when Nigel Lawson and I at that stage suggested a meeting with the Prime Minister, who denounced us for creating a 'squalid conspiracy', or something like that. So independent advice can be useful provided it is exercised in good faith, but it can take quite a lot of time to use it properly.

Since none of the economists, or indeed yourself in the March 1981 budget, would have known that the economy was actually on the turn as you said in that quarter, is it perhaps fairer to say that the 364 economists were unlucky rather than wrong?

No, the central point of my thesis is that they were wrong. The fact is that the economy, as it turned out, was just at the bottom at that time. I was unwise to say in August that the recession was over, which is the kind of thing chancellors ought not to say until they are much more sure than I was then. The fact is that our policy was being governed at that time by the inescapable need to cover our borrowing, and our failure to increase taxes enough made it more difficult to manage that task for the rest of the year. So, whatever we had known about the precise state of the economy, we were being driven by market necessities.

Looking back over the last twenty-five years one can identify a few seminal decisions made by chancellors. You are responsible for three of them: your first budget and the big switch from direct to indirect taxation, the ending of exchange controls and then the 1981 budget. This Chancellor has been responsible for at least one, the decision to give the Bank of England independence on monetary policy. Was that decision, which I believe in

1997 you supported, although Kenneth Clarke did not, ever discussed actively at the time that you were chancellor between 1979 and 1983? We have heard from Nigel Lawson about his attempts to persuade the Prime Minister of the wisdom of that move, but you didn't refer to that.

I think that the points that I did make (which were actually canvassed in *The Right Approach to the Economy*), making it more open, bringing the governor more up front, was about the limit of what we could accept at that time. I don't think we were pressing for revolutionary change beyond that at that stage. I don't remember discussing it as a serious option, and it is extraordinary that interest rate changes were regularly a matter for discussion between myself, the Governor and the Prime Minister, and questions such as the date of the next by-election often were billed as important as other monetary considerations, which is why chancellors like to get it out of Number 10.

Did the appalling social consequences of your policies ever occur to the Cabinet of which you were a member?

I think that some such issues manifestly did, because the social consequences were the consequences of the problems with which we were having to deal. The central point of what I was saying is that it was not possible to escape from endemic inflation on that scale without facing the rise that we did face in unemployment – but it enabled us, with our other policies, in the end to achieve growth and the ability to attack the social policies as well.

How was it, then, that when Mrs Thatcher was eventually driven from office the British economy was in the worst recession since the 1930s?

Well, you will have to ask Lord Lawson about that!

Do certain aspects of the current Chancellor's policies remind you in any way of the sort of policy framework that you inherited from Labour? Do you think that's a reasonable question, given all the criticism we hear about?

I think that it is dramatically different in the sense that the healthy macro-economic growth is continuing. The scale of public sector borrowing hasn't yet been producing symptoms of the kind that we faced in the late 1970s.

If I were to criticize the present Chancellor, the thing that worries me most is his apparent insensitivity to complexity in taxation and legislation. I have been campaigning since before I became a member of the Thatcher government for a sustained attempt to simplify our tax structure, to simplify tax policy as well as tax legislation. Nigel and I were able, between us, to get rid of a lot of taxes, such as development land tax, capital transfer tax, and investment income surcharge, and to achieve some simplification. I got rid of reduced rate bands and saved 1400 people employed in the Inland Revenue and many, many more in the private sector. I think there is huge scope for doing that, which requires enormous patience. Much of what the Chancellor has been doing in pursuit, very often, of legitimate social objectives seems to me to be moving in the opposite direction.

I plead guilty to some tax complications. In my toughest budgets I introduced bright ideas like the Business Expansion Scheme and the Business Start-Up Scheme. Most of them turned out to be shelters for tax avoidance at a later stage without achieving their purpose and they complicated the tax system. I am now presiding over the Tax Law Rewrite Committee. We are rewriting tax law in simplified language. We're not allowed to simplify the policy. I think there is nothing more important in the world. An American writer about this said that, even in the Garden of Eden, if the serpent had offered either Adam or Eve a tax simplification policy it would have gone much further than the apple ever did.

What is your view of the importance of income from North Sea oil, which amounted to something like 5 per cent of GDP?

I think it had two impacts, one gradually of course to provide us with a growing flow of revenue of that kind as long as it lasted, but also to raise the value of the pound awkwardly. One of the reasons for abolishing exchange controls was to counter that. It probably also gave us a period during which it was much harder for traditional manufacturing industries to survive against a high exchange rate but did encourage them to make the adaptations that were necessary. So, like almost every economic development, it brought some plus points, and some minus.

You said at the outset that you were trying to avoid theological absolutes, but surely monetarism is or was a theological absolute. Could I also remind you that you did abandon the Medium Term Financial Strategy in 1985, therefore bringing into question the whole theology of monetarism. The second point I would like to mention is you did describe the situation in the economy at the end of your period as being characterized by success in terms of long-term growth and so on, but you didn't really stress the recession of 1979–81, 3 million people unemployed, and the following recession in 1991–2, with a massive decline in output and national income and again 3 million people unemployed.

I did address and acknowledge the unemployment during my time at the Treasury as being inescapable. It was a consequence of having to get inflation under control, and the absence of it, as we went through the 1980s, was an achievement of success in that direction. For me the sadness is, and I say this in my own memoirs, that by the end of the 1980s we had begun to over-believe in our own success. At that time I was foreign secretary, and I remember making speeches around the world which made it sound as though we had learned to walk upon the water. We became over-confident. That is one of the hazards, and it is one of the hazards that the present Chancellor may face. If he goes on proclaiming as often and as loudly as he does about his economic success, he might begin to believe it himself and land himself with the same problem.

I would like to address much more directly your discussion of monetarism and theology. I have tried to emphasize that I am not a theologian. I am not an absolutist, and I think those who proclaim either monetarism or Keynesianism as 'isms' in which you have to believe are profoundly misguided. Those who have helped us to understand the importance of monetary policy as a component of economic planning have played an invaluable and inescapable role. One of the people whom I admired very greatly during our years in opposition was Gordon Pepper, one of the most regular commentators on the monetary aspect of economic policy, and he taught us to recognize it as important. In the Heath government it was never mentioned in all the debates about prices and incomes policy.

Gordon Pepper has written an interesting book since then with Michael Oliver entitled *Monetarism under Thatcher: Lessons for the Future*,[15] and he there does really try to analyse it in almost theological terms because he categorizes monetarists by degrees of belief in monetarism. Denis Healey in a way started that by talking about sado-monetarism, but he practised monetarism himself. He introduced economic monetary management into his lexicon and was right to do so. To denounce sado-monetarism was to use a quasi-religious device to denounce other people's management of the same economic essential. Gordon Pepper divides people into sheep and goats. He says Denis Healey and Douglas Wass were self-confessed sceptical monetarists. He describes Peter

Middleton, Nigel Lawson and myself rather remarkably as political monetarists. He describes Terry Burns incomprehensibly as an international monetarist, and the only true believers in monetarism, in Gordon Pepper's analysis, are Margaret Thatcher and Keith Joseph – who were, of course, the two who were furthest from the coal face.

Now, I do not believe in monetarism. I am not required to believe in economic doctrines. I attach great importance to monetary policy. I attach great importance also to the learning of Keynes, but they have to be married together and judged. That is why I commended my experience as an assessor of expert witnesses – and economic experts are as difficult as they come.

You briefly mentioned step-by-step reform of the British labour market and labour law in the 1980s, which I took to be a reference back to, and a contrast with, the big bang approach of the Industrial Relations Act. I wondered if there were other ways in which, in labour market reform, you learned from the failure of the Industrial Relations Act in which you were intimately involved.

I don't accept the failure of the Industrial Relations Act. Had we been a shade luckier in the 1974 election the Industrial Relations Act would have survived with very little change. We were adopting a high risk policy, but in a way we had been invited to do so by the breadth of the agenda that Barbara Castle introduced in 'In Place of Strife'. During the late 1960s Stephen Abbot, Robert Carr and I studied the whole of the experience not just of the

United States, but of Canada and other Commonwealth jurisdictions, and produced in the Industrial Relations Bill what was a comprehensive and well-considered package. We were undertaking what the United States had undertaken in the 1930s, 1940s and 1950s, and it was a huge mouthful. But had we not lost the 1974 election, which we lost because of the prices and incomes policy, we would have been able to maintain the Industrial Relations Act, and we should have saved a decade in terms of transformation of our labour market. Having been through that mill, we adopted a much more step-by-step approach in the 1980s. We might have been wiser to do that in the 1970s.

Paul Volcker argued that he brought in monetarism in order to allow him to raise interest rates, which is what he wanted to do in the first place. He couldn't persuade the FOMC [Federal Open Market Committee] to raise interest rates, so he brought in a monetary target and put it in front of them and said, 'There you go, we need to raise interest rates to meet this.' Does that sort of analysis fit in to how you approached monetarism in that, because the targets were being missed and you wanted to get inflation under control, that gave you the ability to explain a rise in interest rates?

You persist in talking about monetarism. I repudiate absolutely this concept of a package called monetarism. You have a more sophisticated discussion of it, I think, in the bulletins from Lombard Street Research. In the last two that Tim Congdon edited there is a much more balanced assessment of the consequences of a Keynesian approach if you take it too far in terms of being automatically linked with incomes policy. I don't believe that, but it is the sort of argument that you can have. I haven't discussed with Paul Volcker why he moved in that direction as he did, but to introduce the need to focus on monetary aggregates as a component of economic planning isn't to adopt a theology, it is to adopt a new aspect of economic measurement and be guided by that as well as others. Do please repudiate this theological approach. I am speaking as a Welshman whose grandfather founded two Welsh-speaking Calvinistic Methodist chapels, so I am full of religious fervour! New economists shouldn't have this kind of religious fervour about them. Reason, reason, please.

If the government and the Treasury had spent more money on an education system that respected intelligence where you got your hands dirty and spent money on leadership skills for management that brought out the best in their workers, might we actually have more of a manufacturing base today?

That is a very difficult question to answer. Education is of fundamental importance, and one could go into a huge debate about whether you need extra resources or not. I don't think I can make the link quite as clearly as you do.

I could begin discussing the financing of university education, but that would be to start an entirely different debate. I merely invite you, those of you who are interested in this, to study a weekly magazine that comes from China called the *Beijing Review*, which discusses the reforms currently being made in the essentially loan-based, fee-based structure of Chinese university education. They describe how they need to have their repayment rates determined by a market assessment of appropriate interest rates. I observe that the two countries that have now got probably the most lively university structures in the world, the United States and the People's Republic of China, are those that are furthest away from ideological opposition to student fees.

Do you think that the economic and social crisis in which Britain found itself in 1979 was the inevitable consequence of Britain's attempt after the war, initiated by the Attlee government, to heal the wounds of the depression and the war? It seems to me you don't believe that. What element of the policies undertaken after the war was, in your view, mainly responsible for this crisis which other European countries, which equally followed economic and social policies based on some social consensus with the union or labour movement, did not experience? What caused the British approach to handling these issues to fail when similar policies in some countries on the Continent did not fail?

I don't really think I can tackle that. It is too comprehensive a question. I think you have to go back and read books like *The Audit of War*[16] and the other Correlli Barnett books to begin to assess the answer. One could cite particular examples. I think, for example, of the comprehensive public ownership of the National Health Service rather than the adoption of the 1944 White Paper, which would have left a much more diverse structure of the health service. That would have been a better approach.

In retrospect the plague of public ownership landed us in a whole range of fool's paradises. It is fascinating that one of the huge burdens that I faced in the Treasury was the wholly unpredictable impact of nationalized industry deficits. They were out of one's control, one found oneself facing a billion pound bill for coal, half a billion pounds for steel. One of the great advantages of liberation in that respect has been to take those chunks off the chancellor's table. Again it is significant that there has been no proposal for reversing any of those changes. That is the really fascinating thing about the history of the last seven years. When Tony Blair secured the removal of Clause 4 and one saw the tone and style of the incoming Labour government manifesto in 1997, I went to the United States two days after the election, and was interviewed by a number of American newspapers. The headline was always 'Top Tory unfazed by Labour win'. I thought that the impact of Thatcherism on the Labour Party had been sufficiently positive to ensure a broadly common ground for the years that followed, and I said in the same interviews that all my life until then I had been terrified that Labour spokesmen might mean what they were saying. My only fear from then on was that they might *not* mean what they were saying.

Notes

1 Edmund Dell, *The Chancellors: A History of the Chancellors of the Exchequer, 1945–90*. London: Harper-Collins, 1996, p. 259.
2 Ibid., p. 454.
3 Ibid.
4 C. H. Sisson, *The Spirit of British Administration*. London: Faber & Faber, 1959, p. 109.
5 In Nicholas Timmins, *The Five Giants*. London: HarperCollins, 2001, p. 254.
6 Bernard Donoughue, *Prime Minister: The Conduct of Policy under Harold Wilson and James Callaghan*. London: Jonathan Cape, 1987, p. 191.
7 Geoffrey Howe, *Conflict of Loyalty*. London: Macmillan, 1994, pp. 125–6.
8 Title of a pamphlet on trade union reform, produced by the Inns of Court Conservative Society in 1961: 'It is excellent to have a giant's strength, but it is tyrannous to use it like a giant': Shakespeare, *Measure for Measure*, Act II, scene 2.
9 Peter Jenkins, *The Battle of Downing Street*. London: Charles Knight, 1970.
10 *The Right Approach to the Economy*, ed. Angus Maude. London: Conservative Central Office, October 1977.
11 John Hoskyns, *Just in Time: Inside the Thatcher Revolution*. London: Aurum Press, 2000.
12 Gordon Pepper, in *Restoring Credibility: Monetary Policy Now*. London: Institute of Economic Affairs, 1982, p. 12, tries to rationalize half a dozen alternatives.
13 Op. cit., p. 481.

14 *The Guardian*, 4 May 1989.
15 Gordon Pepper and Michael Oliver, *Monetarism under Thatcher: Lessons for the Future*. Cheltenham: Edward Elgar, 2001.
16 Correlli Barnett, *The Audit of War*. London: Macmillan, 1986.

4

Changing the Consensus

Lord Lawson of Blaby

The preamble to this book by a clutch of recent chancellors promised that 'Each speaker will shed light on the challenges faced during their time in office and provide a personal account of how these were tackled.' Well, yes, up to a point. Most of us have already done this in our published memoirs, and there is, I think, little point in going over the same ground again. I propose to stand back a bit and reflect more deeply, both on the lessons of those years and, in the light of my experience as chancellor, on the conduct and limits of economic policy in general. And to make sense of it I begin, not from the start of my own chancellorship in 1983, but from the coming of the Thatcher government four years earlier, in 1979.

For that was the watershed, in which I was deeply involved as financial secretary to the Treasury under Geoffrey Howe for the crucially important first two years of the new government, from 1979 to 1981, and my own subsequent six-year tenure was essentially a matter of continuing and further developing the new approach to economic policy in this country on which we had embarked. For what we were engaged in was nothing less than changing the consensus about the proper conduct of economic policy; and that is something that cannot be carried out overnight: it requires at least a decade to achieve.

The circumstances in which we took office made the task both more difficult and less difficult than it might have been. It is hard to recall now the depths to which Britain had sunk a quarter of a century ago. Economic growth, outside North Sea oil and gas, had long been lagging behind that in the rest of Europe and, in the most recent cycle, had virtually ground to a halt: in the despairing words of the Bank of England's March 1978 *Bulletin*, 'Now condemned to very slow growth, we might later even have to accept, if present trends continue, declines in real living standards.'[1]

Inflation was in double figures, and still rising. Management had all but ceased to manage. Increasing trade union militancy, culminating in the so-called Winter of Discontent of 1978–9, had raised the question on all sides of the political debate of whether the country had in fact become ungovernable. Pitied abroad, where Britain had been largely written off by other governments and the financial markets alike as the terminally sick man of Europe, we were mired in an all-pervasive defeatism at home. It was clearly not an easy inheritance.

Yet there was one important sense in which the task with which we were faced was eased. For the inheritance was created not by one government or one political party. It was the result of the cumulative failure of the consensus that had shaped the conduct of economic policy by all governments, virtually ever since the war. It was clear to a demoralized official Treasury that that consensus had been tested to destruction, with the result that, although senior officials were sceptical, to say the least, of the new course we decided to chart, they had no alternative to offer. And it was clear to the public at large that things had become so bad that unpalatable medicine probably had to be swallowed if the patient was to be cured.

Essentially, the framework of the new approach consisted of three interconnected principles, each of them a reversal of the post-war conventional wisdom, as I subsequently set out in my 1984 Mais Lecture, a year after I became chancellor.[2]

The first principle was that the recipe for economic success is the greatest practicable market freedom within an overall framework of financial discipline. By contrast, the approach that culminated in the debacle of the 1970s had in practice consisted in an ever-increasing erosion of market freedom, accompanied by the progressive abandonment of financial discipline.

The second principle was that, instead of seeking to use macro-economic policy – in other words monetary policy to the extent that this existed at all, but essentially fiscal policy – to promote growth and employment, and micro-economic policy (of which prices and incomes policy was the central component) to suppress inflation, we should do precisely the reverse. That is to say, the government of the day should direct macro-economic policy, pre-eminently in the form of monetary policy, to suppress inflation, and micro-economic (or supply-side) policy, such as tax reform, labour market reform, deregulation, privatization and the promotion of competition, to provide all the other conditions most favourable to improved performance in terms of growth and employment.

And the third principle was to set all this explicitly within a medium-term context. The most obvious formal expression of this was the Medium Term Financial Strategy (MTFS). But behind the MTFS there lay a more profound reversal of the old post-war consensus, according to which the overriding object of the chancellor's policies was a largely vain quasi-Keynesian attempt to eradicate, or at least greatly diminish, the vagaries of the typical business cycle, about which policy-makers can in reality do very little, and to focus instead on the conditions for improved economic performance over the longer term, about which history, both here and throughout the world, teaches us that a great deal can be done, even though it can take a while for the results to become apparent.

How, then, did all this work out in practice, particularly of course during my own watch? Needless to say, not perfectly: there were a variety of problems and setbacks, alarums and excursions on the way, all of which I recount in my memoirs. The most painful of these came towards the end, with the so-called Lawson boom of the late 1980s, which brought with it a regrettable resurgence of inflation, albeit to well under half the level from which we had brought it down. This was essentially a consumer credit boom alongside a business investment boom, at the heart of which was a housing bubble which had been exacerbated by the once-for-all effects of financial deregulation. With hindsight it is clear that monetary policy should have been tightened earlier than it was. But with the best will in the world, there is no way in which the monetary authorities can fine-tune bank lending, any more than they can fine-tune expectations.

As Keynes pointed out in *The General Theory*, 'A boom is a situation in which over-optimism triumphs over a rate of interest which, in a cooler light, would be seen to be excessive.'[3] Nor, of course, is there any way the authorities can predict the point at which the credit cycle is likely to turn of its own accord – or a bubble to burst – although turn it inevitably will.

Matters were complicated in the second half of the 1980s first by the unreliability of the official statistics, which persistently seriously underestimated the strength of the boom, and then by the Wall Street crash of September 1987, when the tightening of monetary policy which had already begun in the UK was reversed here, as elsewhere, amid fears that the crash heralded a world recession. Moreover it should be recalled that, throughout 1986 and 1987, inflation was running at some 3 per cent a year – too high for comfort, but not in itself threatening.

I hope the statistics on which the Bank of England nowadays makes the sophisticated short-term forecasts on which its interest rate decisions so substantially depend are of a better quality than those on which I had to rely. But even if they are, it is a myth to suppose that even the most capable of monetary authorities can ensure that the path of economic activity at all times follows a straight line.

For the sake of completeness, I must not leave out the proposition advanced by some that the problem was caused by my decision, in the wake of the Louvre Accord of February 1987, to maintain an informal exchange rate link between sterling and the Deutschmark – the period of so-called shadowing the Deutschmark, which ended in March 1988 – as a proxy for Exchange Rate Mechanism (ERM) membership. I do not believe this stands up, not least because, as Friedman famously pointed out, monetary policy works with long and variable lags. We have to go back earlier, to 1986, when monetary conditions had inadvertently been eased by the sharp fall in sterling, for the period when – with hindsight – we can now see that policy became inadequately tight.

Most of those who point the finger at the 'shadowing' episode do so out of a distaste for any kind of fixed exchange rate. I have considerable sympathy with them, in the sense that, in the long term, rigidly fixed exchange rates are an economic nonsense. But to get inflation down, it helps to have a form of monetary discipline that enjoys a modicum of market credibility.

By the mid-1980s domestic monetary targeting had clearly lost that credibility – nor was it helped by bitter internecine strife among the simon-pure monetarists themselves as to which kind of money, broad or narrow, mattered, or, indeed, if nothing short of full-blooded monetary base control was any use at all. Moreover, history has clearly shown that an external discipline can indeed acquire market credibility.

The gold standard undoubtedly enjoyed it during the conspicuously successful period up to the First World War, but that era is gone beyond recall. Bretton Woods, too, enjoyed market credibility for a number of years after the Second World War, but that era, too, is gone beyond recall.

In the mid-1980s, when I was looking for something to replace the distinctly shop-soiled practice of monetary targeting, the ERM, of which the Deutschmark was the anchor currency, had come to enjoy considerable market credibility, and I believed that a period of this external discipline would assist in the final stages of eradicating inflation and inflationary expectations – as, indeed, it undoubtedly assisted France. But that era, too, is now gone beyond recall. The mishandling of the economic consequences of German reunification, which occurred soon after I had left office, severely damaged the ERM; but the death-knell was the Maastricht Treaty, which effectively replaced it with the essentially political project of European Monetary Union – the single currency – leaving a vestigial ERM merely as an antechamber to EMU, with no market credibility at all.

Today, market credibility has been secured by entrusting the conduct of monetary policy to an independent Bank of England, far and away the best decision that Gordon Brown has taken, which has done an excellent job over the past seven years. As many of you will know, this was something I sought to do in 1988, but was unable to persuade Margaret Thatcher to agree, and launched into the public debate in my resignation speech in October 1989.

Presentationally, Margaret had a point. Inflation, which as I mentioned had fallen to 3 per cent in 1986 and 1987, was on the way up again in 1988, although the Treasury forecast at the time was that it would peak in 1989 and then resume its downward path. But the forecast was uncertain (and indeed to be proved badly wrong), and independence granted at that time might have looked, as Alan Budd recently noted, as if the Bank was being asked to succeed where politicians had failed.

As it was, thanks both to the severe monetary tightening I instituted during my last year in office and to the policies implemented by my three successors, John Major, Norman Lamont and Kenneth Clarke, inflation, having peaked at some 9.5 per cent in 1990, did indeed resume its downward path, hovering around 2.5 per cent during the four years 1993–6. By 1997, when Gordon Brown took office and very sensibly immediately gave the Bank operational independence, it was down to 2 per cent (I have throughout used the Consumer Prices Index in terms of which the Bank's target is nowadays defined).

Thus the Bank's task was not that of getting inflation and inflationary expectations down, but the much less difficult one of keeping them down – a task it has carried out with great skill, and acquired in the process a valuable track record. It has done so, incidentally, without any reliance whatever on monetary targeting. It has, of course, an inflation target; but that is a different matter altogether – not least because an inflation target when you are already there or thereabouts enjoys a credibility which would have been entirely lacking in the difficult circumstances of the 1980s.

As Mervyn King has put it, the past ten years have been the 'nice decade', 'nice' standing for 'non-inflationary consistently expansionary'; and this has been true not just for the UK but for most of the developed world. The next decade, he rightly suggests, may not be as 'nice' – and certainly not as nice and easy.

But there is one fundamental respect in which the world today is very different from, and very much better than, the world we knew in the 1980s and earlier. The coming of globalization – or, rather, the second coming, since it was the condition of the remarkably successful half-century between the end of the American Civil War and the outbreak of the First World War, a period rightly dubbed the *belle époque* – the coming of globalization, as a result of the worldwide move to freedom of capital movements (where this country, incidentally, was something of a pioneer), coupled with the emergence of China as a major player in the global economy, has not only improved world growth but, crucially, made the world economy a vastly more competitive marketplace than it was before.

And there is nothing like an increase in competition to facilitate the task of preserving stable prices. (In parenthesis, I would add that monetarists do themselves no favours by moving from the correct judgement that inflation is caused by the excessive printing of money to the false assumption that monetary authorities engage in this out of stupidity, venality, or just for the hell of it, rather than in response to pressures in the real world.)

Be that as it may, in the context of the thesis of my remarks here, the important lesson of this experience is twofold. First, the fundamentally new approach we put in place in 1979, and persisted with thereafter, did indeed succeed in eliminating inflation where the old one had conspicuously failed; and it was this success that led naturally to institutionalizing it by entrusting the conduct of monetary policy to an independent Bank of England with an unequivocal remit to maintain price stability. Second, the fact that this important institutional change was enacted by the other political party in a two-party system is clear evidence that, at the macro-economic level, the consensus had indeed changed.

And at the micro-economic level, I believe that – despite some regrettable backsliding, notably in the spheres of taxation and regulation – the consensus has also unequivocally changed. The old notion that the promotion of growth and employment should be undertaken via a neo-Keynesian policy of budget deficits has been universally discarded, and the contrary proposition to which we doggedly adhered, that this was the proper and exclusive object of micro-economic policy, essentially through enabling the competitive capitalist market economy to work better, has in effect been adopted by New Labour. Again, this occurred because the new approach – involving deregulation, tax reform, social security reform, labour market reform, privatization and the rest – so clearly worked, as indeed was recognized throughout the world.

I do not wish to enumerate the multitude of measures we took in this context. In Isaiah Berlin's terms, macro-economic policy is the province of the hedgehog and micro-economic policy that of the fox. That is to say, macro-economic policy is one big thing, whereas micro-economic policy consists of a myriad of for the most part relatively small things, which cumulatively become very important indeed.

But if I had to chose between the two achievements of Geoffrey Howe's time and mine – getting inflation down and reforming the supply side of the economy, both of which were of course essential – I would say that the second was the more difficult and thus the greater of the two. I do so on the basis of a simple test. Throughout most of Europe, the 1970s were a worryingly inflationary decade. Yet although the details varied from country to country, every established member of the European Union has succeeded in getting inflation down.

The 1970s also saw the European economy become increasingly sclerotic and underperforming. Yet though our partners on the Continent gradually reached the same conclusion as we had done, or at least paid lipservice to it, namely that the essential remedy was a fullblooded programme of supply-side reform, to remove rigidities and enable the market to work better, for the most part they have failed to get very far, finding it too unpalatable or else too difficult.

It was only after I had ceased to be chancellor that I discovered that, some twenty years ago, Hayek, that great ornament of the London School of Economics before the war, when asked to say something about his differences with Keynesian economics, had replied in these terms: 'Keynes, against his intentions, had stimulated the development of macroeconomics. I was convinced that not only his particular conclusions but the whole formulation of macroeconomics was wrong, so I wanted to demonstrate that we had to return to microeconomics.'[4] In practical political and public policy terms that is a great deal easier said than done. But it is important that it is done; and important, too, to recognize that what it does not mean is a shift of emphasis from government macro-management to government micro-management.

The 1980s, then, were a period of fundamental change in the conduct of economic policy. But there were two important respects in which the nature of the job of chancellor did not change at all in my time, nor is it likely to do so. If the Treasury were to have an institutional motto, it would be the single word 'No'. For at the heart of the Treasury's roles and responsibilities lies the tedious but essential task of the control of public expenditure. It is this that puts the chancellor at odds with most, if not all, of his colleagues, and which makes his – if he is really doing his job – the loneliest job in government.

I suspect I was the only chancellor since the war to have presided over a substantial reduction in public expenditure as a share of GDP. It was this which enabled me to eliminate the PSBR and achieve a budget surplus, despite significant cuts in rates of taxation. It was a time-consuming business, in which I was enormously assisted by a succession of four able Chief Secretaries (Peter Rees, John MacGregor, John Major and Norman Lamont), by the steadfast support of the Prime Minister, and – last but not least – by the high quality of the official Treasury. One of the greatest joys of being chancellor (a job which, you may or may not be surprised to learn, is not all joy) is the exceptional calibre of the great majority of Treasury officials.

The other unchanging – and rather less well-understood – aspect of the job is connected with the task of public expenditure control, but transcends it. Unlike the case in most other countries, the Treasury is much more than a finance ministry. It is also, both in name and in reality, the central department, which means that the chancellor, like of course the prime minister, but unlike any other minister, has a finger in pretty well every pie the government of the day bakes.

While this no doubt stems principally from the fact that there is a public expenditure dimension to most government policies and an economic dimension to almost everything, it is entrenched in the UK by the customary conventions and procedures of government, which I have no reason to believe have changed. To take just one example, no minister may put a proposal to Cabinet without first submitting it to the Treasury, which has the right to insert a paragraph dissenting from all or part of the proposal, and explaining its reasons for doing so. Thus, while as chancellor my direct responsibility for supply-side reform lay in the important areas of tax reform, financial deregulation, and the privatization programme, for which the Treasury had overall responsibility, I was also able to take advantage of this central role to become deeply involved in those aspects of supply-side reform in which the Treasury was not in fact the lead department. But though, again, a time-consuming business, this aspect of the job of chancellor is, I believe, important to any administration which desires to ensure what I would call policy coherence and what seems to be known nowadays as joined-up government.

But while much has stayed the same, much, too, has changed. I have already noted how the wider economic environment has been transformed by the second coming of globalization and, within that context, by a large part of the third world – and not just China – embracing the market economy and, happily, making unprecedented economic progress as a result. Indeed, there is now almost a sense of terror in some quarters of the richer world that some of the poorer countries are becoming rich at our expense, leading to a resurgence of protectionist sentiment which it is essential to resist.

But along with the new global economic environment there have come new challenges, too. Let me mention just two of them, one which is itself global in nature, and the other which is a particular challenge to this country.

The first of the two new challenges which I wish to touch on is the threat of climate change, or global warming. This is an area where Her Majesty's Treasury has an important role to play, and so far as I am aware is failing to play it.

That global warming is a major challenge we have on the authority of no less an expert than the present Prime Minister – who, it has to be said, has something of a penchant for apocalyptic warnings based on flimsy evidence. But insofar as there is any hard evidence of global warming as a secular rather than a cyclical phenomenon, it comes from the steady increase in so-called greenhouse gas emissions from the growing consumption of carbon-based energy in order to fuel global economic growth. And the likely future rate of global economic growth is a matter on which economic expertise is more relevant than any other.

The likely rate of global warming is as important as whether or not it is occurring. Mankind has shown itself to be astonishingly adaptable, and the market is a remarkably successful institution for harnessing that adaptability. But, clearly, the more rapid the rate of climate change, the stronger the case for government intervention in this area. So a dispassionate economic assessment is badly needed. Yet so far from undertaking this, the Treasury seems to be content to leave the matter entirely in the hands of what used to be known as the Department of the Environment, nowadays the Department for Environment, Food and Rural Affairs (Defra), which of course has a vested departmental interest in maximizing the gravity of the threat.

This is why the Treasury's traditional role as the dispassionate and objective central department, not merely in the field of public expenditure but more widely, has always been considered so necessary. Yet it seems that over global warming it has entirely abdicated that responsibility, even so far as the essential task of cost–benefit analysis is concerned. For if the costs of action taken to reduce global warming exceed the benefit from the extent to which global warming is reduced, then clearly such action should not be undertaken.

The Treasury's apparent abdication is all the more serious because Defra, in turn, has largely contracted out the analysis of this important issue to an international quango, the Intergovernmental Panel for Climate Change, or IPCC, which not only has an even greater vested interest in maximizing the scale of the threat and thus its own importance, but which has shown a determination to suppress or ignore dissenting views and reasoned criticism that is little short of a scandal.

This is, in fact, part of a wider problem. It is, I believe, no accident that it is in Europe that climate change absolutism has found the most fertile soil, for it is Europe that has become the most secular society in the world, where the traditional religions have the weakest popular hold. Yet people still feel the need for the comfort that the transcendent certainties of religion can provide, and it is what might be termed the quasi-religion of greenery which has filled the vacuum, with reasoned questioning of any of its mantras regarded as a form of blasphemy. I hope I am not alone in finding this mind-set profoundly disquieting, as well as economically harmful.

Unlike global warming, the other new challenge facing the Treasury and the chancellor is, as I have indicated, a matter for this country alone. It is, of course, the question of whether we should join the European Monetary Union, and exchange our own currency for the euro. So much has been written about this that I will do little more than indicate where I stand.

It is no secret that European Monetary Union is a political and not an economic project. In the first place, in an age of globalization, the economic context is global rather than regional. And in the second place, in purely economic terms there can be little dispute that the imposition of a single monetary policy over an area as large and diverse as the European Union, with its many different languages, cultures and traditions, is undesirable.

How much economic damage it is likely to cause to the various peoples of the Union over time is difficult to predict. In normal times the cost may not be very great, although it is of course cumulative; but circumstances could arise – the so-called asymmetric shocks – when the harm would be considerable. This is the overriding economic consideration, which none of Gordon Brown's celebrated five tests really touch.

The Treasury is, of course, well aware of this: hence the proposal buried away in the voluminous study of British euro membership it published in 2003, and which was subsequently promoted by the chancellor's chief economic adviser, that the problem could and should be addressed by reverting to neo-Keynesian fiscal fine-tuning. Sadly we have had more than enough experience of fiscal fine-tuning in this country to know, not only that it does not really work, but that it inflicts considerable micro-economic damage.

So the question, essentially, is whether it is in our national interest to pay an economic price of uncertain magnitude, coupled with the political price of giving up a major element of self-government, in return for the undefined political benefit of being 'at the heart of Europe' – not that EMU membership alone would put us at the heart of Europe anyway. It clearly cannot be.

Of course there are some who find the whole concept of national interest objectionable. In an age of globalization, it is argued, the nation-state has become an anachronism. History provides the simplest refutation of this muddled thesis. The late nineteenth century is widely recognized as having been the heyday of the nation-state. Yet it was also, as I have already mentioned, the epoch that saw the first coming of economic globalization. Others argue that, whether or not the nation-state has in fact become obsolete, it certainly ought to be, given the havoc that nationalism has wreaked over the past hundred years.

Now, there are three great forces that make the weather that governments have to steer through. These are self-interest (including the interests of one's children), nationalism and religion. Each of them can certainly turn ugly, but each of them can also be a force for good. (It makes no more sense to reject nationalism *tout court* because of its evil exploitation by Nazi Germany than to reject religion *tout court* because of the excesses of militant Islamic fundamentalism.)

So far as self-interest is concerned, Adam Smith long ago demonstrated how the market economy channels this into public benefit. But nationalism is important, too, in this context. It is no historical accident that the evolution of the nation-state and the evolution of the market economy coincided. For the market economy rests on a non-economic infrastructure, of which a vital component is the rule of law. And in a free society, the rule of law will work satisfactorily only if the people feel that, in the last resort, it is their law.

The rediscovery of the market economy is not by any means the whole of the new consensus I have made my principal theme, but it is its most important component. There is nothing ideological about the market. I admit, personally, to placing a high value on individual freedom; but there are other important values, too. The dominance of the market economy in the world today is essentially Darwinian: a matter of the survival of the fittest, as rival systems have been tested to destruction. There are good reasons why this should have been so. There is the great benefit of competition, which only the market can fully provide. There is the Hayekian point that the market is an unbeatable signalling system, providing and diffusing the information required for rational business and consumer decisions on a scale to which no other system can remotely aspire. These are both compelling reasons; but to my mind the most compelling of all is that the most fundamental fact of economic life – as indeed of other dimensions of life – is that we are all fallible.

We all make mistakes and we always will. Markets make mistakes, and so do governments. Businessmen make mistakes, and so do politicians and bureaucrats. Thus any attempt to construct an economic system which will eliminate mistakes, or even some kinds of mistake, is doomed to failure. All we can sensibly do is put in place a system in which mistakes are soonest recognized and most rapidly corrected. And that means, in practice, the liberal capitalist market economy. By contrast, experience shows that, whatever the political system, it is governments that find it hardest to own up to mistakes, still less to correct them.

All this is so obvious that it is puzzling that Britain, which invented the market economy and, in Adam Smith's *Nature and Causes of the Wealth of Nations* (the full title is so much more significant than the customary abbreviation), first explained it, should have taken so long after the war to rediscover it. A large part of the explanation can be attributed to the influence of that towering polymathic intellect and forceful personality John Maynard Keynes. Keynes was essentially a Platonist, believing that government policy – including not least economic policy – should be determined by a properly educated and selflessly public-spirited intellectual élite. (This remains, incidentally, the ruling tradition in France, which explains the rooted French distrust of the market and a significant part of the French élite's instinctive hostility to the United States.)

Thus Keynes believed that investment decisions should not be left to what he described in *The General Theory* as 'the uncontrollable and disobedient psychology of the business world' but should to a substantial extent be determined by government. Nor should capital flows be left to the market: as he wrote, only five years before his untimely death in 1946, 'Nothing is more certain than that the movement of capital funds must be regulated.'[5]

One insuperable problem with economic Platonism, however, is that there are never going to be many paragons of the kind specified by Plato in the *Republic*, or any guarantee that they will be in government. There are not even many Keyneses, in every way about as close to the Platonic model as we are likely to find in the real world. And Keynes himself was distinctly fallible. In particular, over-influenced by the experience of the 1930s, he came to the mistaken conclusion that slump was almost the natural condition of free economies. It was this error which provided much of the intellectual underpinning of the inflationary disaster of the 1960s and 1970s.

But there is perhaps an even more fundamental misconception. Economists, at least since Marshall, have mistakenly sought to dignify their calling by describing it as a science, and have increasingly chosen to add verisimilitude to this pretence by clothing their propositions in the language of science, that is to say, mathematics. Despite being a one-time mathematician myself, I doubt if any chancellor of the Exchequer has ever been assisted in the slightest by a mathematical equation. For economics is not a science.

On scientific matters we rightly expect a high degree of certainty, and are ready to leave many important decisions to properly educated experts. By contrast, economic policy, while undoubtedly a serious subject, is more like foreign policy than it is like science, consisting as it does in seeking a rational course of action in a world of endemic uncertainty. It is to cope with the realities of this sort of world that the new economic consensus, which came into being during the course of the 1980s, is so much better fitted than the old. It will not guarantee that the decisions that are taken will always be proved right. But it makes it much more likely that the worst errors will be avoided. And no one can ask more than that.

Questions and Answers

From your experience as chancellor, Lord Lawson, what is your view about the value of having at Number 10

Downing Street a group of advisers to the prime minister checking, supervising and advising the prime minister about the work of the Treasury?

I think it is perfectly reasonable for a prime minister to have his or her own personal economic adviser, just as he or she may want a personal adviser on foreign policy. I don't think you need a group, but a personal adviser who is independent from the Treasury, I find this perfectly reasonable. I have always thought that, but it is important that it should be in private. When a personal adviser starts going public, so that it becomes unclear as to what the economic policy of the government is, then I think it is distinctly unhelpful. But provided it is private advice given frankly, and you can have an internal discussion if there is a difference of views and thrash it out, I think it is thoroughly healthy.

In your lecture, Lord Lawson, you referred to the quality of the Treasury civil servants but you also referred to very serious errors in forecasting, and from my recollection Denis Healey made exactly the same point. That seems a paradox. Is it a paradox and, if so, can you explain it?

There are different explanations possible. One of them perhaps is that short-term forecasting is impossible, so that even the cleverest and most industrious people fail. I think it is very difficult, and it is one of the reasons why one needs as much as possible to have a policy which doesn't depend on forecasting. Nevertheless, as you see from the Bank of England's inflation report and the minutes of the Monetary Policy Committee, forecasts have to be used. I think it is sensible for those who are using them to be very sceptical and to be aware of the quite appalling track record forecasters have had. But in monetary policy perhaps it doesn't matter quite as much as elsewhere in macro-economic policy. If you get your forecast wrong it is rather easier to reverse monetary policy and avoid further damage than is the case in most other areas.

You alluded to the Louvre Accord in passing. You were very heavily involved in the Plaza Agreement and the so-called Plaza 2. If you were chancellor now, would you be getting involved in a Plaza 3, given the imbalances in the world economy, or would you leave it alone?

I think in the world we now have I would leave it alone. It is very difficult to answer categorically, because I haven't given it as much thought as I would have done had I been in office, but I think in the world of today it would be very difficult to make something of that kind work. It is not because I have some objection in principle. I think for a short time it can be helpful, but I think it would be very, very difficult to do something that worked. Therefore it is better not to attempt it.

I just wanted to make sure I understood you clearly in terms of your views about whether it would have been better to have an independent Bank of England in the late 1980s or essentially whether, with the benefit of

hindsight, taking Alan Budd's thesis, to which you alluded, it is now your view that it was OK to use the ERM to bring inflation down? The reason I ask the question is because if one looks around the world and looks at other inflation targeting countries like Australia and Canada, New Zealand and so on, they managed to switch to inflation targeting, switch to an independent central bank, and brought inflation down with a very small rise in unemployment. The sacrifice ratio was rather better than the sacrifice ratio that eventually happened in the UK, which used the ERM.

I came to a very clear conclusion in 1988 and said that we would do well to move to an independent central bank. I tried very hard to persuade Margaret Thatcher but was unable to do so at the time. I published in my memoirs the memorandum that I sent her at the time setting out what I believed would be sensible.

What I was acknowledging, however, was that she had a political point, namely it would have reflected badly on the government because it would have looked, and this was Alan Budd's point, as if the central bank was being asked to succeed because the politicians had given up. That would have reflected badly on the government. Whether it was sufficient reason not to do it in 1988 is arguable. In any event it would have taken time to get the legislation through. But it certainly could have been done a great deal sooner than 1997, no doubt about that.

Can I ask you a question about tax policy, which you didn't cover in any great detail. One might have argued until relatively recently that another part of your changed consensus, in addition to the roles of macro-/micro-policy, was a view that the best thing the Treasury could do on the taxation system was to make it as simple as possible. You abolished a tax in every budget and it appeared there was a consensus that complicated systems of allowances were a bad idea. In the last seven years we seem to have completely reversed on that and the Treasury has become much more interventionist, with a lot more tinkering. Is it true that that element of the consensus has gone under this Chancellor?

There is clearly some continuity. I brought the top rate of income tax down to 40 per cent in 1988, and it has remained at 40 per cent ever since. I am quite sure that if I hadn't brought it down then it wouldn't be at 40 per cent today, so some things have endured. One always hopes that what one does will endure, not merely for the good of the country but also because it is pretty hard work to have everything you've done reversed by the next government! But you are absolutely right on the other part. The idea of tax simplification and having no loopholes, and as few tax breaks as possible, whether they are accidental ones which clever accountants have discovered or whether they are ones deliberately introduced by the government of the day, is a good one. You want low rates but with no exceptions, and there has been, I think, a very sad reversal on that front, you're quite right. It is very much for the worse. I hope that sense will come back. I hope it is not a permanent reversal.

You mentioned the credit boom that occurred in the late 1980s and the high expectations for income and the house price rises that went with that. I wonder if you have any insights for what's going on in the market for credit and houses now, drawing on your time.

I suspect it is similar but not the same. It is not the same because, although history always does repeat itself, it doesn't repeat itself in an identical way; there are always different features and different contexts. Secondly, in the late 1980s there was a huge business investment boom, sometimes forgotten because the consumer credit and housing boom was so big and such an obvious talking point at the time. The business investment boom was partly a consequence of deregulation, particularly big bang and all that, which meant a whole lot of international banks and other financial companies were coming to London. There was a huge explosion of business investment in the financial sector and, of course, when you get that sort of mood, other businesses start investing more, so you have the two things going on at the same time.

We are not getting a business investment boom at the present time. It is just a consumer credit boom and in particular a housing boom. So I suspect there is going to be a bursting of the bubble, indeed maybe it is already getting deflated. I cannot predict how far it will go; nobody can predict these things. That's why there will always be a cycle, because in a free economy you can neither predict nor control it.

I suspect it will be different and less serious than it was in the late 1980s, partly for the reason I have already given. But there is also another reason which may be even more important. The 1980s formed the first cycle in which people had been free to take their own decisions. Financial deregulation changed the picture enormously. Hitherto what had happened was that consumers wanting credit, whether it was for purchasing houses or for any other reason, were to a greater or lesser extent rationed by the banks or the building societies. They in turn rationed credit because the government was to a considerable extent controlling them, partly by statutory means, such as the so-called corset, and partly by leaning on them. So they were accustomed to looking to the government to take their decisions for them.

In the late 1980s everybody was suddenly liberated. Not only did consumers not feel the need for self-discipline, which you do need in this free framework, but unfortunately neither did the financial institutions, who really went mad. I am not saying they should have been helping the government; they should have been helping themselves, because it was they who by their folly incurred all the bad debts, which took a long time to work through. So this was the first cycle in the post-war era of freedom and I think people have learned from that. Not totally, people never do. People are only ever really able to learn fully from their own experience; they never learn as much as they should from the experience of previous generations. But they have learned something.

Would economic management be improved if the prime minister and chancellor of the Exchequer were one and the same?

You might as well have a dictator deciding everything. No, I don't think for a moment that would help. It is possible for chancellors and prime ministers to work very closely together. It may not look like it at the moment but it is possible. During the vast part of my time as chancellor I worked extremely closely and very happily with Margaret Thatcher and there was absolutely no problem at all. The problems only arose towards the end. I think prime ministers don't need to be particularly interested in this area. Margaret Thatcher was of course passionately interested in monetary policy. I don't think the present PM is interested in the slightest, so you do need a chancellor of the Exchequer, and I am speaking in a totally dispassionate way because I am not applying for the job in any future government.

This sounds terribly conservative, but I do think that the system we have in this country where the role of finance minister and the role of the economics minister, including the control of public expenditure, are both under one department and one minister is very much better than that in many other countries such as the United States, where for example the control of public expenditure does not come under the Treasury. In many European countries you have a distinction between the finance minister and the economics minister, and you have one responsible for taxation and the other one responsible for public expenditure. Well, of course, there has to be some kind of bringing together of the two sides of the national accounts, so the fact that we put all that in one department with one minister is better for what is nowadays known as joined-up government – but what, being old-fashioned, I call policy coherence. But I would not merge numbers 10 and 11 Downing Street.

You were talking about the supremacy of market efficiencies, and I just wanted your view on the structural adjustment policies of the World Bank, in particular advocating liberalization of agricultural markets. Do you think there is an element of hypocrisy on the part of the Western world in the view of the agricultural support policies in place in the US and Europe?

I am not in favour of protection at all, and I have made many speeches, including when I was chancellor, attacking agricultural protection in the United States and the European Union and indeed Japan, where in many ways agricultural protection is the worst. You do your best to fight that, but that doesn't mean it is hypocrisy to urge countries to open up their markets if you think that's to their benefit. I'll say two things about globalization which bear on that in totally different ways. One is that if you look at those third world countries, to use an old fashioned expression, which have opened up in a sense to a global economy and those that have decided not to, then it is absolutely clear that those who have opened up, for all the difficulties, have fared far better than those such as Cuba who have turned their backs on the global economy.

The other connection is that globalization has meant that you're no longer, as a developing country, dependent on World Bank money in the way that these countries used to be, because there is a huge, far bigger, private capital market which you can access if you are pursuing policies which have the confidence of the markets. So that I think is good news. Globalization is very good news for the third world in that way.

You talked very persuasively about the consensus, but I am wondering if there is not a downside that I might just refer to. For instance, when one travels around European countries one is struck by the quality and the efficiency of the infrastructure in contrast to that in the UK at present. I am wondering whether you might say that was the case partly because of the reduction of public investment here in the 1980s and 1990s. Also what would you have to say about the manufacturing catastrophes that occurred in that period?

I'll say three things if I may. First of all, the grass on the other side is always greener. I live half my time in France nowadays and half my time in England, and I wouldn't do that if I didn't love living in France. But you know they have all sorts of problems too and they are very happy to talk to you about them over a glass or two of wine. The train service does run on time but there are many fewer lines and many fewer trains. It is a different way of approaching it. As for their health-care, I think it is a better set-up than the much more socialist health-care set-up we have in this country. But it is a major problem if you read the French press: it is creaking at the seams and they are hugely worried about what to do about it.

Second, the under-investment in the railways was an under-investment which occurred well before privatization, well before the 1980s. There had been a history of under-investment there because it was a nationalized industry, and the dead hand of the Treasury was not in favour of spending money on it if it could avoid it. So I don't think that is a criticism of the new consensus.

Finally, manufacturing: there is nothing special about manufacturing. What you want is a successful economy, and if manufacturing firms are finding it harder because the third world is doing more and more in manufacturing, whereas in the service sector there is huge growth, I don't think that's a disaster. In fact if you try to resist that change you're being very silly.

Towards the end of your speech you poured scorn on the idea of economics as a science and you mentioned foreign policy as well. I have been thinking about this. Is it not the case that any action, whether in economic policy or in foreign policy, presupposes some set of cause and effect relationships? These relationships are presupposed, and isn't it the job of the social sciences, including economics, to make these implicit relationships explicit and to test them as far as possible? This may or may not mean that you can have an open mind on which methods will prove successful. Actually in international relations there is a far greater range of models and a far greater range of approaches than is nowadays used in mainstream economic institutions. Discuss!

I am tempted just to say 'yes', which I think is what your question deserves, but I don't want to be unkind. What

I would say is that I think the best way of understanding these relationships is not through mathematical equations. What you put into the model is what you get out of it anyway. The best way of understanding these things is to understand economic history. I greatly regret that when I read PPE at Oxford many years ago, and I was primarily a philosopher, I was obliged to do two economic papers, economic theory and economic organization. There was no economic history paper at all, unless you specialized in economics and did it as a special subject, an optional extra, and I think that probably in this country – maybe the LSE is totally different – not sufficient time is devoted to economic history. You learn about these relations far better in that way. It is almost as if, in politics, you studied political theory and political institutions but no political history, which would be ludicrous. It is equally ludicrous I believe in economics.

With all due respect, Lord Lawson, don't you feel that on the euro topic you misrepresented the issue slightly by saying Europe is a completely political union and by downplaying the economic effects of the euro in two ways? You say it is an inevitable failure due to the huge differentiation between European countries when in fact nation-states which have huge differences, like China and the United States, run successfully on a single currency. Secondly you misrepresented it by saying that you lose the ability to set monetary policy when in fact you lose the ability to set an interest rate, while the Bank of England would retain cash ratios, deposit ratios, even

their own bank regulations. Do you not feel there is more to be said about this topic?

Listening to a talk by you is a bit like hearing a speech by Gordon Brown in terms of the consensus because he's always talking about the progressive consensus that he says he's created now of high health and education spending and redistribution to 'hard working families'. Just to stop us all agreeing, can you say, if you had had his inheritance, what you would have done differently?

I didn't quite understand the relationship you drew between the Maastricht Treaty and the end or demise of the ERM. Maybe you could elaborate?

A number of different things. As for what I would do in Gordon Brown's position, I indicated in an earlier answer that I would certainly not have complicated the tax system in the way that he has. The way in which you get improved productivity – he's right to say that in the 1990s we had higher productivity in this country – is not to try and micro-manage the economy, it is to get a framework in which businesses can perform and are likely to perform and are stimulated to perform better.

The two questions about Europe. The Maastricht Treaty point is quite a simple one. The framers of the Maastricht Treaty, Jacques Delors and others, claimed that we had to have a single currency because the EMS was no longer sustainable. When they said that, they themselves didn't believe in it any more. It clearly rapidly lost market credibility. I think market credibility would have diminished as the size of capital flows was increasing, but certainly when, for political reasons, they said that, inevitably, this is no longer sustainable and we have got to move to a single currency, clearly this no longer had any credibility. So that's the connection, which I think is a fairly obvious one.

As for whether I mis-stated the position, no. Everyone on the Continent of Europe accepts that this is a political issue. There is nothing disgraceful about being political. I was a politician myself. But let's be open about it, let's not have any subterfuge. There is not just one political agenda because different countries involved in it have different political agendas, but it is political. I may not share the political agenda, say, that the French have even though I love France. Equally one may feel that it is unequivocally not worth paying an economic price in order to secure this presumed political objective. That is the point, and I don't believe there is any mis-selling about that.

Notes

1   *Bank of England Quarterly Bulletin*, March 1978.
2   Mais Lecture, City University, 1984.
3   John Maynard Keynes, *The General Theory of Employment, Interest and Money*. London: Macmillan, 1949.
4   *Hayek on Hayek*, ed. Stephen Kresge and Leif Wenar. London: Routledge, 1994.
5   Op. cit.

5

Out of the Ashes

Lord Lamont of Lerwick

The day that I became chancellor of the Exchequer in the last week of November 1990 I went into the Treasury, into that very long dark room that was then the chancellor's office, and met Terry Burns, who was then the Chief Economic Adviser. He said to me, 'Chancellor you do realize you will soon be the most unpopular man in Britain?' That was the only Treasury forecast in my time that was ever correct.

I don't think even Terry quite realized how bad things were going to get. I remember several years later, after I had stopped being chancellor of the Exchequer, I got in a taxi and the taxi driver said to me, 'Mr Lamont, I saved your life!' And I said, 'How's that?' He said 'Well, I was driving up St James Street one day and you were crossing the street and a man in the back said, "Five hundred quid if you run the bastard down"!'

Sir Samuel Brittan, the distinguished writer and political economist, wrote recently in the *Financial Times*: 'Who now remembers the ERM?' Well, I wish it were like that! He went on to say, 'But mention it to a politician and you'll get a shudder.' Well, I do intend to mention the ERM, because one of the things I have discovered is that I am now an exam question.

I first found this out when my two children were doing A-levels. I also discovered something else. We are all as politicians used to finding, like any individual is who is reported or written about in the newspapers, that anything that appears about us in the newspapers is wrong. What I had not realized was that anything that appears about you in a school textbook is wrong as well. But it is very flattering to be an exam question.

I remember once, in 1991, I received a piece of paper through the post. It was an exam question and at the top was written: 'University of Reading'. It was from the Department of Sociology, and there were a number of questions. One section was on the sociology of humour, and question 15 was 'Which chancellor of the Exchequer used humour to the best effect? Winston Churchill, Lloyd George or Norman Lamont?' And I thought, 'Oh, that is very flattering,' and then I looked at the date of the exam question and the date was April 1st.

There are many things that I could mention here. I could just touch on the Treasury as an institution, about life in the Treasury. Denis Healey did that, and he went out of his way to say that he did not really care for the Treasury civil servants, and preferred those in the Ministry of Defence. By chance I had lunch with him today, and I said to him, 'You know you were echoing Winston Churchill', because when Winston Churchill became chancellor of the Exchequer he wrote complainingly to a friend: 'All these chaps here speak Persian. I prefer generals and admirals'. I liked the people in the Treasury, and I liked the Calvinists of the Inland Revenue. In my book I described the charms of the old building of the Treasury before Gordon Brown turned it into a 'Hyatt Hotel'. The old Treasury had wonderful wide corridors with red linoleum and double swing doors, and I wrote that it reminded me of a Russian psychiatric hospital. One always expected the doors to swing open and a trolley to come by with some unconscious patient. Malcolm Rifkind, when reviewing my book on my time at the Treasury, said, referring to my description of the Treasury as a psychiatric hospital, 'Norman Lamont has confirmed what many of us have thought for a long time about the inmates of the Treasury'.

I could mention the Private Finance Initiative (PFI), which is one of the things that still looms large in discussion and arguably has been somewhat misused. I could hold forth about the Maastricht Treaty, which took up a very large part of my time at the Treasury. That was the treaty from which I negotiated the opt-out for sterling, but it was the treaty I did not want to sign and did not sign in the end. Mercifully somebody did it for me. Or I could discourse about the process of budget-making. It is quite an interesting subject in itself and I could talk about the three budgets I had the privilege of presenting. The first of them drew the sting of the Poll Tax while we were still inventing the Council Tax. My second budget was on the eve of the 1992 election, which put one in an impossible position. It was the most political of all my budgets, and it completely wrong-footed Labour, who were not sure whether to oppose or support a low rate band because of its appearance of help for the lower paid. Looking back on it, it was not a very good budget. But it did help us to win the 1992 election. My next budget, my third budget, helped to lose the 1997 election for the Conservatives, but it was definitely my best budget.

Before I come to the ERM I would like to say that I have to refer to events before my time and also after my time. Nothing should be interpreted as criticism of anyone who has spoken before me in this series of lectures or anyone who is going to speak subsequently. Kenneth Clarke is a wonderful person, sound on everything except the euro.

The ERM today has no friends, and it is widely regarded as a disaster, although there have been a few dissenting voices. The other day Sir Samuel Brittan wrote a piece in the *FT* saying that it was too soon really to come to a final verdict. And Sir Alan Budd, the Provost of Queen's College, Oxford, who was the successor to Terry Burns as Chief Economic Adviser at the Treasury, in his Wincott Lecture wrote: 'The case can be made that the ERM was an economic triumph and marked a turning point in our economic performance.'[1] It is worth recalling that the decision by John Major to join the ERM in October 1990 was one that was greeted with euphoria in the press, by the CBI, even by the stock market, which rose 60 points on the day. Joining the ERM dramatically increased the stature of John Major because he had succeeded where Nigel Lawson and Geoffrey Howe had failed. He had persuaded Margaret

Thatcher to drop her long-standing opposition. How he did it is a mystery to me, but he must have had some secret gift that convinced her, against her long-standing instinct, to change her mind.

My own attitude was ambivalent. I was not involved in the decision to join. There was a very pre-emptory announcement at Cabinet. I was told just twenty four hours before the decision was made. My own attitude towards fixed and floating rates was one of agnosticism, though with a bias in favour of floating. The day we joined the ERM I met a senior civil servant in the Treasury and said to him, 'What have we done this for?' And he replied, 'Oh for political reasons.' I replied, 'Well, I don't think I would like to have given up the flexibility of the exchange rate.' I never imagined at that time that this decision was going to be one that would have such consequences as it subsequently did.

The attractions of the ERM for its advocates developed out of the experience of other counter-inflation policies. The Conservative Party that came to office in 1979 was determined to reduce inflation, which when we came to office was around 15 per cent. Attempts to control inflation by setting quantitative targets for the money supply in the early 1980s had not been entirely successful. Even if inflation came down it owed much to the rise in the exchange rate as well as to monetary targets. There were arguments that continued about what was the proper role for the exchange rate. Some argued that one should fix interest rates and the exchange rate would take care of itself. Others argued that this could not be allowed, because of the impact of the exchange rate on the price level. It was not inevitable that the exchange rate should necessarily go up, it might go down, with adverse consequences for inflation. But in the early 1980s sterling was allowed to float freely. It appreciated, with severe consequences for exports but beneficial consequences for inflation.

At the time advocates of the ERM argued that, if we tied the pound to low inflation currencies and set interest rates accordingly, British inflation would fall to the level of the best. This is what Edmund Dell dubbed 'exchange rate monetarism'. In 1985, Geoffrey Howe and Nigel Lawson attempted to persuade Margaret Thatcher to join the ERM as a way of buttressing monetary policy. She rejected this but in June 1989, after a lot of argument, ministers agreed amongst themselves the so-called Madrid Conditions for joining the ERM. These included the abandonment of exchange controls within the European Union, increased competition in various areas, and lower inflation. The last was probably the most important condition, but was one that was not met when we joined the ERM. Inflation in October 1990 was at the surprisingly high rate of 10.9 per cent.

It should be noted that this interest in fixed exchange rate regimes wasn't confined just to Europe. In other parts of the world also, in Asia and South America, monetary authorities were finding it difficult to run independent domestic monetary policies. There were many different regimes of pegged exchange rates with the dollar, or currency boards, both in South-East Asia and in South America.

The main characteristic of the ERM was a regime of fixed exchange rates that linked our currency to the others in the system, the key one being the Deutschmark, the linchpin of the system, in which we were linked at the central rate of DM2.95 to the pound, with fluctuation bands of 6 per cent on either side.

Even some people who supported the ERM did not appreciate fully how it was meant to work in practice. Interest rates remained the main tool of monetary policy, but now the overriding factor in setting them was to meet the UK's ERM obligations and to keep the pound close to its central rate against the ERM currencies. This wasn't some additional discipline but a complete regime for interest rates. The consequence for a high inflation country, as we were at the time, was that interest rates would have to be higher until our inflation rate moved into line with that of the best, which was that of Germany, the anchor of the system. Indeed from the moment we joined the ERM, our interest rates were heavily influenced by those of Germany.

The conditions when we joined the ERM, and we joined the ERM about eight weeks before I became chancellor of the Exchequer, could hardly have been less suitable. Firstly inflation was 10.9 per cent, secondly we were entering a recession. Just before I became chancellor the monthly unemployment rate had risen by 32,000, the highest figure for four years. John Major at the time as chancellor was reluctant to use the R word 'recession'. When I became chancellor it was pretty clear to me that we were in a recession and I used the word immediately, although there was an argument about how long it would last and how deep it would be.

Subsequently people came to believe that the ERM caused the recession, but it did not. It was already under way when we joined the ERM. The recession was inevitable because we had high inflation and before we joined the ERM we had had high interest rates, firstly 13 per cent and then 15 per cent for a whole twelve months in 1989–90.

The history of the next two years is all too familiar. The recession lasted for a year and a half, through to the second quarter of 1992. Housing repossessions soared, bankruptcies soared, unemployment went from 1.7 to 2.8 million. All this time I featured in *The Sun* newspaper, alternating with Graham Taylor, the manager of the English football team. Sometimes I was the turnip and sometimes he was the potato and sometimes it was the other way round. I have never met Graham Taylor. I have got great admiration for him: I feel we have got a lot in common. One day I would like to meet him.

I remember *The Sun* at that time produced a strange cover. I was taken out to lunch by a senior journalist on the newspaper and he gave me a lavish lunch and then handed me a page for the next day's edition. It had a huge dartboard with my face in the middle of it, which was going to be the front page. As he gave it to me he said, 'There is nothing personal in this.'

The pressure on me was to talk up the economy. One colleague in the Cabinet wrote to me and said, 'If you just say there'll be a recovery, there will be a recovery.' If only it had been that simple! I was determined to be realistic and was criticized both for being too pessimistic and by others for being too optimistic. Looking back on it, my reference to 'green shoots' was not quite as ill-timed as people then thought; Gavyn Davies subsequently called it 'remarkably prescient'. But my wife quite rightly asked, 'How can you have green shoots in the autumn?'

All the time there were calls for interest rate cuts, from the CBI, from the press, from members of Parliament, but we could only deliver them slowly. People often forget that during our membership of the ERM we actually cut interest rates all the time. Other than on 16 September we never increased them. I remember the look of horror over John Major's face when I remarked to him, 'One day we might have to put interest rates up.' But we cut them from 14 per cent in October 1990 to 10 per cent in September 1992. That had to be done carefully because we always had to keep the market hungry. We didn't want to snatch at it. Above all we had to have regard to our position within the bands.

The problem was that, although interest rates were coming down, inflation was coming down faster, so real interest rates were rising quite sharply. When we joined the ERM inflation was nearly 11 per cent and interest rates were 14 per cent. By September 1992 inflation was just under 4 per cent and interest rates were still 10 per cent – a real interest rate, if you measure it against the RPI, of around 6 per cent. Even if we had wanted to cut interest rates faster, we couldn't have done so under the system. As Sir Alan Budd put it in his Wincott Lecture, 'Norman Lamont in the role of Ulysses was tied to the mast.' The *Financial Times* had a wonderful misprint. It said: 'Norman Lamont in the role of Ulysses was tied to the mast, his *eyes* stuffed with wax so that he was unable to hear the siren calls of reflation.'

The basic problem in the ERM was, as became gradually apparent, the contrast between the needs of the German economy and those of the UK economy. This became greater as time went by. Germany was enjoying a construction boom following reunification in 1989. During our membership of the ERM we started off with inflation as the main problem, but the UK moved deeper into recession, and inflation receded. The UK needed lower interest rates, Germany needed higher interest rates, though Germany's inflation was low compared to what our own had been.

In December 2001, this contrast between the needs of the two economies and the constraints on our ability to get rates down became very marked. Germany, far from cutting rates, started putting them up. It meant that for the period from September 1991 to May 1992 UK interest rates remained unchanged at 10.5 per cent, although inflation in May 1992 was 4.3 per cent. At that time I did feel like Ulysses. I really did feel tied to the mast.

A few months after that the wax in Ulysses' ears became a little bit looser and I began to hear some of the siren calls, particularly after the second German rate increase in July 2002. I came increasingly to believe that we were going to have overkill on inflation, that inflation was going to be driven down at the expense of recovery. I debated this endlessly with officials in the Treasury, all of whom, with one exception, were strongly in favour of soldiering on. I remember one civil servant put it quite bluntly to me. 'This policy', he said, 'was decided by the present Prime Minister, the previous Prime Minister and the Foreign Secretary, and you've been here less than two years and you think you can change it. Are you sure you have the right to do this, just to give up when it is proving difficult?' I was not convinced and I tried to persuade the Prime Minister that we should indeed consider suspending our membership. He would not entertain it and I accepted his decision. That was the end of the matter. I little saw what was about to hit us.

Another complication with the ERM was the connection between the ERM, the euro and Maastricht. Many people, but not I myself or Nigel Lawson, saw the ERM as leading in an evolutionary way towards the euro. As the result of the Maastricht Treaty that had been negotiated, France was due to have a referendum in the third week in September on Maastricht and the euro. The market sensed that the French might say 'No', and speculation built up. The markets had this fixed date against which to speculate. Initially the currency in the front line was the lira, and the speculation built up with the date as the point around which it centred.

The pressures continued. On 8 September the first domino to go was Finland, which had its currency tied to the ecu. The Finns floated the markka, having lost a huge part of their foreign exchange reserves. After them came the Swedish krona. Mortgage rates went up 5 per cent in a week; overnight rates went up to 75 per cent. Then on 11 September the lira fell out of its band and was devalued by 7 per cent. At the time I didn't think that the 7 per cent would do them much good, and indeed it did not. It was not the end of their agony; there was a second devaluation and then the Italians floated.

The pound was not helped by remarks to a newspaper by the Bundesbank President, Dr Schlesinger, which he called 'unauthorized', where he had said he thought the pound was overvalued. He made these remarks on 15 September. I was at dinner that night at the American Embassy. I spent a lot of time trying to persuade Robin Leigh Pemberton, the governor, to persuade Dr Schlesinger to withdraw these remarks. Dr Schlesinger kept just saying, 'They were unauthorized.' But he would not actually withdraw them.

I expected 16 September to be a very difficult day, and it indeed it was. By 8.40 that morning we had lost £1 billion out of the reserves. The story of the rest of that day is well known. At 10 a.m. I put interest rates up to 12 per cent. I remember sitting in the Treasury watching the screens, waiting for the news of the interest rate decision to come through. Sterling was flat, just outside the bottom of its band. The screen just did not move when interest rates went up. I felt rather like a doctor watching a heart machine and having to conclude that the patient was dead. Unfortunately I had a lot of difficulty in persuading my fellow ministers in the Cabinet that the patient was clinically dead. I recommended to John Major that we should leave the ERM immediately. He wanted to consult other ministers. We spent a long time discussing this. I and the Governor recommended several times that we should leave the ERM, but ministers wanted us to put rates up further, in a final attempt, to 15 per cent, which had no effect. The decision to put rates up to 15 per cent was the worst decision of the day, and it meant that the haemorrhaging of the reserves went on and on.

I would just like to make one important point about the 'losses' to the reserves. Much of the press afterwards concentrated on the loss of the reserves. But they did not distinguish between decisions to support the pound, so-called intervention about which I was always sceptical, and payments out of the reserves which we were obliged to make. The greatest part of the loss of reserves did not come from discretionary decisions, futile attempts to support the pound. We were not chucking money around trying to support the pound. But under the system of the ERM, once the currency is outside its bands, people could buy sterling, come to the Bank of England and demand to be paid at the official parity. It was a licence to print money at that moment between 10 o'clock when we refused to get out and the early evening when we finally did.

I felt, I have to say, a certain relief when it had all happened. It is not true to say, as was reported endlessly, that I sang in my bath, any more than it is true that I ever said 'Je ne regrette rien' about economic policy. But I did feel a degree of relief about it because I did feel that we were embarked on a different path and the future would work out well.

Of course there were widespread calls for my resignation. I considered that option, but I did not resign really for two reasons. Firstly the Prime Minister asked me not to and secondly colleagues said to me that if I did it would certainly just shift the pressure to him, who was the architect of the policy. He told me he saw me as his air raid shelter. In any case, whether that was right or wrong is arguable. But I have to say that I was glad that I stayed on for another eight months because it gave me an opportunity to reconstruct policy on an entirely new basis.

I think it is worth emphasizing that the ERM crisis was an international one. I described earlier what happened in Finland and Sweden. I am always surprised at the extent to which people see it purely as a British crisis. In that week in September 1992, eight countries either devalued or floated. These eight countries lost a large part of their foreign exchange reserves at that time. There was another country, France, which a few months later had a delayed crisis and was forced off its central rate, having spent, according to newspapers, 150 billion francs trying to support the franc within the ERM.

Later the tide of speculation moved on to other fixed rate regimes outside Europe, in Asia: the Thai baht, the Malaysian ringgit, and the Korean won. I remember the Korean Minister of Finance was put in prison and impeached. I was rather alarmed by this at the time!

Could we have avoided the situation and the crisis which hit us? Well, there are a number of questions that need to be addressed. First of all there is the issue of whether we joined at too high a rate. I know many people believe that to be the case. I cannot shed any light on why the rate of DM2.95 was chosen. Plainly it was a demanding one, but I was always told it was simply the inflation adjusted average over the decade before. I was amused to hear that Mr Delors was reported to have said that he didn't mind what rate the British had as long as it wasn't the one they wanted.

I am not convinced that the rate was too high when you look at the subsequent behaviour of sterling. It went down below 2.50 up to 1987, but from 1997 until quite recently it was much nearer 2.95, and on some occasions it has been over the 3 Deutschmarks. Secondly, should we and could we have devalued? I do not believe that would have helped because the real problem for output and employment was not the level of the exchange rate, it was the level of interest rates. Had we devalued but tried to remain within the system, we would have had to pay a premium on interest rates. Indeed those countries which in September 1992 did devalue but remained within the system had to pay a price in terms of higher interest rates.

I want to talk now about the reconstruction of policy. But before I do that could I just say what I think about the experience and the benefits and disbenefits of our membership of the ERM. It was dramatically successful in forcing inflation down within a very short space of time, from 10.9 per cent to 3.6 per cent on 16 September 1992. For the whole of 1993 inflation was below 2 per cent, which was the best inflation performance for thirty years. It was a really decisive break with inflation. For the whole period of the government of Mrs Thatcher the average annual inflation rate was around 6 per cent. Whenever we seemed to have finally got on top of it, it bobbed up again.

Was policy too tight? Well, I admitted the contradictions in my own mind. I am conscious of the contradictions as I speak to you. In the summer of 2002 I became concerned about the tightness of policy, and yet, as Alan Budd has asked, 'too tight for what?' Too tight possibly for output and employment, but not if one wanted to get inflation down to genuinely low levels, to German levels. Inflation was not just knocked on the head by the ERM, it was slain.

Could this objective have been achieved by other means? Making the Bank of England independent perhaps? I was attracted to the idea of making the Bank of England independent and I did twice try to persuade John Major, but he was not interested. In fact I do not think we could easily have achieved the same result with an independent Bank of England. A newly independent Bank of England operating a very tight money policy against the conditions that existed could only have done so if there was a consensus about what needed to be done. I did not believe an independent Bank of England would have survived the sort of criticism and public outcry that there was against the level of interest rates we had within the ERM. All the vitriol that was, understandably perhaps, addressed against the ERM and me would have been addressed against a newly independent Bank of England, and its independence would quickly have come under attack.

Could we have operated a discretionary policy which would have had the same result? After all, interest rates were at 15 per cent for a whole year up until we joined the ERM in 1990. I know politicians, and I know the politicians I was working with. I know myself. I described the doubts that even I had at various times, I do not think that we would have persisted long enough to get the full gains of low inflation. As it was, whether we wanted them or not, we did get them. Without the ERM discipline we would have relaxed interest rates probably when inflation had got to 4 per cent or something like that. Don't forget there was an election looming in 1992.

What we often forget when we joined the ERM was that we did not only just give up the right to choose our interest rates, we also effectively gave up the right to choose our inflation rate. The system implied having the German inflation rate. My view is that we got benefits from being a member of the ERM and we got the benefits from leaving, though the latter was obviously a matter of luck. Had we continued, inflation would have been driven too low and we would have had a very anaemic recovery. The ERM was a tool that disintegrated when it had outlived its usefulness, but the effects both of being in and then of leaving worked to our advantage. People say, yes, we got the benefits when we left. But I think the benefits when we left could only happen because of the benefits that we had when we were in.

After we left the ERM interest rates could be cut much more aggressively, and were cut in one-point steps down to 6 per cent in January 1993. During this time I had to reconstruct policy. My new policy was announced to the House of Commons Treasury Select Committee on 8 October 1992.[2] It consisted of an inflation target, the institution of regular monthly meetings with the governor, and regular inflation reports. This regime has worked remarkably well. It is essentially the regime that the independent Bank of England operates on today. It was further built on by Kenneth Clarke, who took the additional step of publishing the minutes of the monthly meetings.

Far be it from me to attack myself, but I am slightly surprised at the brilliant press it has had. David Smith in the *Sunday Times* called it 'the most brilliant piece of policy-making in the post-war period, the basis of the stability we enjoy today'. Sir Alan Budd, in his Wincott Lecture again, said, apparently without a trace of irony, 'it is universally acknowledged the current framework for monetary policy is as close to perfection as fallible men can hope to achieve.' I hope you will forgive me for quoting this. I looked in my own book to see what I wrote about the inflation target, and unfortunately I devoted only half a page to it!

I am pleased that the inflation target has worked well, but this is not the end of history. Anatole Kaletsky and Patrick Minford argued that what I did was as important as the fact of the Bank's independence, i.e. the targeting was more important than the independence. Flattered as I am, I am not sure I would go so far. But I think the independence of the Bank of England and the framework I established enabled the benefits from the ERM to be made permanent. We could not have had an inflation target before we had got inflation down to really low levels.

My last act as chancellor was the budget of 1993. The recession had played havoc with the public finances. I introduced a savage budget. It was really three budgets in one because I did not just announce tax increases, I legislated for tax increases for the next three years. As Peter Riddell wrote in *The Times*, 'It really doesn't matter who's chancellor for the next three years.' Those tax increases totalled £17.5 billion. The most unpopular of all was 17.5 per cent VAT on fuel and power, for which I think there was and is a perfectly logical and coherent case. I was sorry that the House of Commons subsequently reduced the rate. The budget predictably was wildly unpopular. The *Daily Mirror* had a picture of me as a blue Eskimo under the headline 'The Iceman Cometh: a cheap and shabby budget from a cheap and shabby man'. *The Sun* called it 'Nightmare on Norm Street'. Anatole Kaletsky called it 'A budget to pay for Norman's mistakes'. Well, it was wildly unpopular but I think it was right. It was the best thing that I ever did, though the main beneficiary was Gordon Brown. He inherited a strong fiscal position, and was able to blame the Conservative Party for the tax increases.

It was all too much for the Conservative Party – albeit the economy had now stabilized, unemployment was falling, and the economy was beginning to grow again as it had begun to do since the second quarter of 1992. In May the Prime Minister offered me another job in the Cabinet, but I felt it would be better if I returned to the backbenches. *The Sun*, on the day I left the Treasury, had a picture of me with my back to the camera, walking away from the Treasury. The headline was: 'The picture all Britain wanted to see'. But I had some consolation. A few weeks later I was walking through Notting Hill and there was a tramp sitting on the pavement, drinking out of a meths bottle. He suddenly raised his meths bottle to me and croaked, 'Mr Lamont, it's all coming right and someone else is getting the credit.'

Peter Jay wrote about my time as chancellor, 'Norman Lamont evidently never believed in ERM membership . . . .' It was a bit more nuanced than that. Peter Jay continued, 'but accepted it as the price of office and lived like Cardinal Wolsey to wish that he had given his convictions as high priority as loyalty to his political master.'[3] I think that is a reference to Shakespeare's *Henry VIII*: 'Had I but served my God with half the zeal I served my King, he would not in mine age have left me naked to mine enemies.' But I know from Lord Irvine's experience that politicians who compare themselves to Cardinal Wolsey get into deep trouble. Peter Jay continued: 'To that extent Norman Lamont's economics were better than John Major's, but his ethics were not. He invited his own tragedy because he who lives by political calculation must expect to die by political miscalculation, as he did just at the moment when he got the economic policy he wanted, which was probably also as close as Britain had been to having a coherent economic strategy for about fifteen years.' Well, I do not complain too much about that as an epitaph.

It seems to me that in politics you often have to compromise, you often have to make difficult choices. Politics is described as the art of the possible, though to me it has always seemed the art of choosing between the disastrous and the unpalatable, and that was the situation for much of the time I was chancellor.

Out of the Ashes

Questions and Answers

Can I take you back to your 1992 budget, which you skated over slightly at the beginning? You could say that not only was it reckless with the public finances but it also, by being so successful politically, left the Tories in the dire political state they're now in by winning that election, which was an election to lose. How do you feel about being characterized as a man who produced such a brilliant political budget that it left the Tories in a dire state?

I don't see how winning the election left us in dire straits, unless you mean we won an election it would have been better to have lost, because if we'd lost it Labour would have had the ERM crisis and Labour would then have had the blame. Look, in reality you cannot choose to lose an election; you cannot deliberately say, 'I don't want to win this election. I am going to go out to lose it because I know what's going to happen.' Frankly, that is incredible.

Can I comment, though, on two points? One about the looseness of the budget. The 1992 budget, looking back on it, was over-expansionary. But I genuinely believed that the modest tax reductions I made in that budget were consistent with a responsible attitude and with a realistic estimate of what the PSBR would turn out to be. I was wrong, but I genuinely believed it. I would never have thrown caution to the winds for the chance to win an election. I thought I had this rather clever wheeze – the lower rate band. I know a lot of tax purists don't like it. But Neil Kinnock couldn't make up his mind whether it was really a tax cut for the poor or whether it was something else, and he didn't know whether to vote for or against it. Actually it was worth it just for the pleasure of seeing that. But it was a modest tax reduction. While I was wrong about the outcome for the PSBR, the margin of error was far greater than the tax cut.

I will say one other thing. When you talked about where the Tories are today, one of the things that is commonly stated about the ERM, rather than the 1992 budget, is that it destroyed the reputation of the Conservative Party for economic competence. I would just like to address that point, because for me it is rather a heavy burden to bear. There are two measures of economic confidence: one of them is by MORI and the other is by NOP. Actually the latter did show that in 1996 and 1997 the Conservative Party in economic confidence ratings was ahead of the Labour Party. If the Conservative Party is now behind the Labour Party in economic confidence, it might be something to do with the perceived competence of the Chancellor of the Exchequer rather than what happened in 1992.

The other thing that is commonly said is that the Conservative Party has 'flatlined' in the polls since 1992. At the back of my book I published all the opinion polls since 1990, and if you gave them to someone from Mars who didn't know when the ERM had happened, they would not be able to tell by looking at the monthly opinion polls when we left the ERM. In January 1993 the Conservative Party stood at 37 per cent in the polls, somewhat above where it currently is, and there has been no flat line. What happened was the Conservative Party gradually fell in a series of steps in response to a whole series of things such as BSE, sleaze, Europe, and most of all the arrival of Tony Blair. The party went down to 22 per cent in 1994 after Blair's election as leader. This whole idea that it has just flatlined since 16 September 1992 is just one of those things that everybody says, but when you actually look at the statistics they don't support it.

It has been in some of the reports that, sometime before the crisis in mid-September, it was proposed as a solution that certain countries, amongst them Britain and Italy, would devalue. But you insisted that every country in the ERM should devalue against the Deutschmark and this was rejected by the French. Would you like to comment on that?

It is true that I would have accepted a revaluation of the Deutschmark. As I have explained, I felt that a unilateral devaluation of sterling would simply leave the UK with higher interest rates. In my opinion the problem for the British economy was not so much the level of the exchange rate, but the level of interest rates. Had we devalued we would have had to pay higher interest rates. Over the whole existence of the ERM, the countries which had devalued had for years – the Dutch for a long time, the French for a while – had to pay higher rates. That is why we were not interested in a unilateral devaluation. We did talk to the Germans about a revaluation of the Deutschmark alone, but the French were absolutely against that as well.

I would like to offer a different view. Departure from the ERM was not a reflection on the Tory Party. The real reflection was on the financial and economic system which caused the government, and all the eight countries which you've mentioned, to lose control completely of what was happening. Foreign exchange trading is a matter of gambling and has nothing to do with interest rates or lower inflation.

Well, I believe in the free movement of capital. I do not believe in controls over capital movements or foreign exchange trading. As long as you have the free movement of capital and no exchange controls, you will have the opportunity for speculation. That is the counterpart of a free economy. I have never had any problem with that. I have even had dinner with Mr Soros – I didn't know I was going to have dinner with him, it was someone's idea of a joke! I certainly don't hold anything against George Soros. He saw an opportunity and he exploited it. No, I think the opportunities for speculation come from governments setting up artificial opportunities for them. So although I am grateful to you I actually don't think it is really the fault of the speculator.

Do you see any parallels between yourself in 1992 and say John Snow [US Treasury Secretary] today and likewise between George Soros in 1992 and the Chinese

Central Bank today? If you do, what kind of advice would you give to the US Treasury today?

I think the situations are very different, because the dollar is floating freely against European currencies. I view the depreciation of the dollar with some concern, but with the public sector deficits and the current account deficit, the depreciation of the dollar is likely to go on. You've got a sort of semi-fixed exchange rate system operating in the Far East and there is a strong case for some of the currencies in the Far East to revalue. But I appreciate their concerns, that, until they have reformed their banking system, complete liberalization may be difficult. The important thing is that America ought to address its deficit as quickly as possible.

You've obviously concentrated on the domestic aspects of the chancellorship, but during your chancellorship we saw the break-up of the Soviet Union. I wondered if you would like to make any comments about that, because you witnessed a lot of that at first hand, what was done and what should have been done.

Yes, actually that took up quite a lot of my time. I was very interested in it and I count myself very fortunate in that I saw a lot, not just of the finance ministers, but of both presidents Yeltsin and Gorbachev. We were able to give quite a lot of technical assistance to Russia, in reforming their banking system, in improving their tax collecting. I remember also very well the privatizations. There is a lot of criticism of the privatizations today and there have been cases in Russian courts relating to them. But I have to say that my feeling at the time was that of relief that these large entities were privatized, even if it was not done in the most transparent way. It was not done with a transparent auction, or with the clearest rules.

I think one has to remember that, after the break-up of the Soviet Union, at one point it really looked as though there was a possibility, I put it no higher than that, of the Communists returning to power. Many of the people who bought assets in the former Soviet Union bought them with that risk. Overnight that risk went when the Communists were not successful. But I have always had the greatest admiration for all those people like Gaidar, whom I got to know well, and Yavlinsky, who leads the Yabloko Party. I have always been amazed at how well those people understood market economics. I once asked Gaidar how it was that he understood free markets. These people understood market economics far better than many people in the West. Mr Gaidar told me that he studied economics while pretending to be study-ing maths, sitting at the back of his lectures reading eco-nomic textbooks. I thought many of the people I met were brave people and achieved a lot.

The macro-economic stabilization in the early 1990s was a brave and bold achievement. We owe an enormous debt of gratitude to Mr Gorbachev, who is somebody I admire simply because he was a man who renounced violence. But he did suffer from the illusion that he could liberalize communism, and his understanding of eco-nomics was not that great. I remember him once asking me how it could be right for an umbrella on the black market to sell for four times the amount it was in the shops. He also thought that privatization would just lead to zillionaires. Of course that's exactly what did happen, I suppose! But he had no concept that privatization could work out in a different way.

Yeltsin, I thought, was very skilful. Russia, it might be said, is not really a democracy, but as in all democracies tough economic measures are very unpopular. Privatization and removing price controls were both very unpopular. Yeltsin was much more committed to economic reform than Gorbachev. He would regularly sack his finance minister and then replace him with another whose views were exactly the same, and reform went on.

Can I just ask, after all the macro stuff, about the personal cost? You came to the chancellorship as the result of having played a pivotal role in the ascension of John Major to the premiership, and you won him the 1992 election. Is it always destined to go wrong between the chancellor and the prime minister?

I think it probably is. I have pondered about this. I think the prime minister is always going to be much more political than the chancellor of the Exchequer. The problem about being Finance Minister is that you are in a minority of one in every meeting. Everybody always wants to spend more money. Everybody always wants to pursue a gradual approach: there is never to be any pain, everything is to be lovely all the time and nothing unpopular should be announced before a by-election or a party conference. Unless the chancellor has the backing of the prime minister, he cannot do his job effectively. Mrs Thatcher always, always, sided strongly with the Treasury, and that is a great advantage for the Treasury.

The advantage that New Labour have had is that Brown and Blair initially operated together, isolating the rest of the government. I was amazed when they stuck to Tory spending plans immediately after the 1997 election. Having spent the whole election denouncing us for wanting to make people homeless and tear down the hospitals with our own hands, they then announced they were going to do that themselves! But the strange thing is that, instead of feast and famine, it has been famine followed by feast.

Initially I believed that the stories about Brown and Blair disagreements were to some extent got up by the press. People put the relationship under the magnifying glass, and then people talk to advisers on both sides. After a while these things take on a reality of their own. It seems to me the Blair–Brown tensions have increased in the first place under the magnifying glass, although there was undoubtedly a tension there.

When we asked these chancellors who had been there from 1974 to you, except for John Major, why they couldn't provide an inflation target, I didn't think they gave very convincing answers. Germany had an inflation target in fact for all that time in the mid-1980s. I cannot see why we did not introduce an inflation target in the mid-1980s which would have avoided the inflation of

the late 1980s, because the eye would have been more firmly fixed on inflation rather than getting muddled up with the exchange rate shadowing the DM or this or that. Wouldn't it have been better to have had an inflation target all along?

It would have been quite difficult to introduce an inflation target when inflation was in double figures because if inflation is high progress towards the target will be gradual. It would take years to achieve a good outcome. I think it was easier to introduce it after we had reduced inflation. We ended up with a good policy almost by accident. First of all we had monetary targets, then we had an eclectic policy that included a bit of exchange rate and a bit of monetary targets, then we had exchange rate monetarism, and now we've ended up with an inflation target on the back of a low inflation rate. As I say, I don't think it would have been easy to introduce an inflation target when inflation was high because success would only have been slow and gradual. I don't believe a government would have persisted with it to a successful conclusion.

I think also one shouldn't regard inflation targeting as an end to all argument about controlling inflation, because it still begs the question as to how inflation is to be controlled. What weight is to be given to monetary policy, what to asset prices, to the exchange rate? All the questions that we'd been through could reappear again under the rubric of an inflation target. I am very pleased that it has worked from 1992 to now, but I don't think, as I said, it is the end of history. I could imagine – I hope

I won't see this, but I could imagine – depending who you put in the Monetary Policy Committee, you might get the wrong answer. You might get incompetent inflation targeting. So I am very flattered that everybody thinks I personally found the answer to all our problems, but I am not sure that I believe it.

How satisfied were you that you were adequately warned by the Treasury both of the difficulties of staying in the ERM and of the dangers, in other words, the economic undesirability of it? Secondly, did the Treasury have a plan of campaign to preserve the ERM parity? How good do you think it was technically?

Let me answer it this way. I did not foresee what happened on 16 September. It hit me in the face, although I did see it after Dr Schlesinger's remarks. How far it was foreseeable you may have your own opinion, but I did not foresee it. Looking back I often think that I should have done, but I did not.

Now the other part of the question: was I warned about the effects on the real economy? Well, I could see that myself, and I was much more alarmed about that than my officials. In a way, I have been trying in my lecture – I plead guilty to this – to get the best of all worlds because I have been saying I was sceptical about the ERM, but it did produce beneficial results. I am as guilty as anyone, but I did see dangers from December 1991 onwards. In the summer of 1992 I made two demarches with John Major. I was worried that if we remained in the ERM a recovery just could not happen –

except a very anaemic one – and I think that was a right judgement. Most of the officials disagreed with me – all but one. They took the view, well he's just a politician, hasn't got the guts to soldier on. But actually I think we would not have had a proper recovery had we carried on, and when I look at the subsequent history of France, and the subsequent history of other European countries, I think we had a 'better outcome'. One of the things that is vividly etched in my mind was the rate cut in January 1993. I cut rates by 1 per cent then, and there was an outcry, particularly from France and Ireland. Bertie Aherne said, 'The UK isn't entitled to solve its own problems.' You could have knocked me down with a feather.

We also did not foresee the effects of German reunification. I have much more difficulty in working out whether that should have been foreseen or not, but that was not foreseen at all. No one warned one in any way about that. But I am not criticizing.

Was there a contingency plan if we were forced out?

I don't think there was a contingency plan. Round about 16 September there was a lot of phoning Helmut Kohl and phoning the Bundesbank, but that didn't do much good, and even if the Germans had made up their mind to try and assist us I don't think it would have made any difference to the eventual outcome. The Germans acted entirely properly within the rules of ERM, but only that and nothing more. It was interesting that in the summer of 1993, when the franc was forced out of its bands, the Bundesbank spent a huge amount trying to support the franc. That in the end was completely pointless, but it is fair to say that there was no contingency plan.

Notes

1   *Black Wednesday: A Re-examination of Britain's Experi-ence in the Exchange Rate Mechanism*, Alan Budd, Wincott Lecture, 5 October 2004, London: Institute of Economic Affairs, 2005.
2   Letter from Norman Lamont, Chancellor of the Exchequer, to John Watts MP, 8 October 1992.
3   Peter Jay, 'The Economy 1990–94', in *The Major Effect*, ed. Dennis Kavanagh and Anthony Seldon. London: Macmillan, 1994.

6

The Quest for the Holy Grail: Low Inflation and Growth

Kenneth Clarke MP

I continue to marvel whenever I come to the London School of Economics that a Conservative politician is now able to enter its precincts without any difficulty. It is not much more than ten years ago when the police had to be called to restore order in one of my meetings, where I was saying nothing that I thought was particularly disturbing. Times have changed. But it is perhaps because I have become an elder statesman that I was invited back to reminisce.

I appointed the current director of the LSE, Howard Davies, as Deputy Governor of the Bank of England shortly after the collapse of Barings Bank. The whole Barings episode had a background of a rather peculiar nature. There was not a great deal for me to do at the time of the collapse apart from taking the key decision that, in my opinion, it posed no systemic risk to the banking system and brought no irreparable damage to the reputation of the City of London. Therefore there was absolutely no case for the Treasury to put in any public money in order to rescue this comparatively small bank, which was a victim of its own errors and had plainly allowed a maverick trader to bring it down.

Nevertheless we had to react to the crisis on the basis that it was a tremendous and pivotal moment, so in Number 11 Downing Street, on the Sunday I think it was, my permanent secretary and I both had to be there, surrounded by young men who were busily trying to act in this crisis on the basis that there was something they could do, which actually at that stage there really was not. All of them were trying to ring up people in the Far East and Bahrain, in order to try to sell them a bank which was currently insolvent and the full extent of whose liabilities were at that stage unknown. They were not getting very far. Firstly it was not possible to raise anybody in the Far East on a Sunday with any great ease, secondly the proposition they were putting forward was positively ridiculous. But my permanent secretary Terry Burns and I were sitting around trying to look important, as though we were in the middle of this great mass of activity. I got rather fed up after a time so I suggested to Terry, who was a very keen supporter of Queens Park Rangers, that as Queens Park Rangers were playing Nottingham Forest on that particular afternoon – there was a Sunday fixture – it seemed to me that we would be just as well employed if we went along to the ground and watched the game. So a rather reluctant permanent secretary was bundled off to the match. I enjoyed the game – it wasn't a particularly good one, but it was certainly more engrossing than listening to other people making unsuccessful telephone calls.

The Quest for the Holy Grail

We of course made it clear that we were imminently at the disposal of the department the moment any activity broke out, and my permanent secretary's enjoyment of the game was somewhat disturbed by the fact that he kept breaking off every five minutes to go crawling on his hands and knees up the concrete steps in order to ring the office to see if there was any news. There was no news, so he might as well have concentrated on the game. It was one of the more bizarre features of my time at the Treasury: an event that appeared to be a crisis but was not really a crisis as far as the chancellor was concerned.

It gives some insight, I suppose, into what the Treasury was like. If I may begin, therefore, with my general views of the Treasury as a department. I do not know what my other four distinguished predecessors have said about it. I have had a much reshuffled career. I have had far more ministerial posts than any of the previous lecturers in this series. From department to department I hawked my wares in the course of our period of government, and I rapidly discovered that every government department had an internal atmosphere totally unlike any other. They might as well be separate fiefdoms in the feudal whole. I had just come from the Home Office, which is about the most reactionary and slow-moving department in Whitehall. It is a very distinguished department but it does not like telling its ministers too much about what it is doing, and above all it does not like ministers trying to change things. It is very, very hierarchical and very slow to move.

The Treasury is, of course, with the Foreign Office the most distinguished of the departments of state. Though it shared with the Home Office the intellectual distinction of the senior principals, it did not share anything else. It had a totally different atmosphere. I ran it as a kind of permanent debating society. I think in that respect my tenure was a total contrast to that of my successor, Gordon Brown, who only speaks to people who agree with him, whereas I am a combative personality who likes debating. Some people would say I like arguing for the sake of it. So very open discussions and arguments took place about every feature of the department in which I was involved. Treasury officials were not remotely resistant to change, and I particularly liked the non-hierarchical nature of it.

I would attend meetings where the officials all argued with each other, something totally banned in the Home Office – and in most other departments – in front of the secretary of state or the chancellor. They would disagree with each other fairly ferociously in their opinions of what should be done: the guy who had just left university would sit there arguing with the permanent secretary with apparently no damage to his career prospects, and certainly not disturbing the atmosphere of the meeting. I always said it reminded me of being in an Oxbridge college, though I suppose I shouldn't say that in the London School of Economics. When they annoyed me I also used to say to them that it reminded me of an Oxbridge college, in that we seemed at times totally out of touch with the real world. It seemed to me to be part of my duty to keep us in touch with reality, but in spite of that it was a very enjoyable department to be in.

My appointment was a bit of a surprise to me. I was settling down to being home secretary. I thought I would be home secretary for the entire parliament, and had my predecessor not gone under a political bus, no doubt that would have been the case. I am sure the police service, the prison service and various other parts of the Home Office were happy to be spared the rather turbulent process of reform on which I thought we were due to embark. I was suspected of being about to repeat what had gone on at the Health Department and the Education Department, and I thought then, and I still think now, that the police service is one of the least reformed parts of the public service in this country. The prison service has not been reformed since the time of the great early Victorian philanthropists, so I was quite determined to have a go at it. I got moved away at an unpropitious time for my predecessor, who found it was impossible to carry on, and was asked to stand down. In a way it was a slightly unfortunate time to enter the Treasury, something I would always have wished to do, but none of the circumstances were quite right just to charge on and put into practice finally the views one might have formed about macroeconomic policy.

The politics, you recall, were slightly fraught. Firstly my party was about to have a civil war, which was warming up very nicely over the Maastricht Treaty and turned itself into a neurotic civil war. The repercussions of that civil war are not wholly over yet. The entire time I was at the Treasury, the background in the House of Commons was that members of the governing party were at each other's throats and steadily tearing themselves apart. It seemed quite obvious to me that we were putting ourselves in a completely unelectable situation as a result, so at least I had a finite period of office to look forward to.

Secondly the immediate background to my arrival had been Black Wednesday and the departure from the Exchange Rate Mechanism, which had led to the complete destruction of the government's reputation for economic competence. One realized it had gone on the day. I do not plan to reminisce at length about Black Wednesday, but I was there, by chance in a way, though I have often said that the fact that Douglas Hurd, Michael Heseltine and I were ostensibly present in Admiralty House for another purpose was simply a way of making sure that we had our hands dipped in the blood in the day's crisis which unfolded in our presence.

The other thing I walked into was a mounting fiscal crisis. We had a very large and very rapidly rising budget deficit, which was confidently predicted to be rising to £50 billion on the way in which we then calculated it – which was altogether more honest and open than the way it is calculated now. That deficit was thought likely to have dire consequences for the economy of a country which had just come through the crisis of Black Wednesday.

In my mind, as I contemplated the situation I was in, I had only one reassuring thought. It did seem to me that if a prime minister sacks a chancellor he cannot sack a second chancellor. The second one has a much better prospect. Barring some absolute disaster, there was absolutely no way in which a prime minister could twice fire the chancellor of the Exchequer. Otherwise the only positive thing about the prospect was that it could only get better.

The key priority was to do what had to be done to try to sustain our recovery from the recession, which had reached its trough only two or three years before, and to try to recover from the consequences of Black Wednesday. In my opinion, our failure to manage fiscal policy properly had played a very large part in our failure to stay in the Exchange Rate Mechanism. All the parties joining the ERM and leaving it have a different theory about what happened. Even some of the people with whom I am in very close agreement on the broad principle of the thing differ on their analysis of our exit. I am not one of those who believes that we went in at the wrong exchange rate, I do not believe it was a disastrous error in the first place. The timing was not ideal but it could have worked.

I believe that we failed during the time we were in the ERM to give proper effect to things we said would be the results of going into the mechanism. We did enjoy declining inflation, we were able to bring down interest rates, but we also talked about how joining the ERM would impose a discipline on governments which hitherto had lacked the will to take tough decisions. We did not put that into practice. We actually promised to reduce taxation and began to do so. We hugely increased the level of public spending and began to forecast a steadily ascending rate of public spending in advance of the growth of the economy. So we began to run into a huge fiscal deficit sometime before Black Wednesday.

I came to the view that, far from regarding the ERM as a discipline, too many of my colleagues regarded it as a kind of escape from reality. We did not need to be disciplined in our management of our economy, because the ERM would be credible in the markets in any event, and anyway we could be rescued if any crisis occurred. Hence in the run-up to Black Wednesday, instead of acknowledging that losing control of fiscal policy might have been a contributor to the problem, my colleagues took the view that it was all the fault of the others for not rescuing us.

If there was any problem in the public finances, well, we could have access to the Bundesbank in order to plug any gaps. In particular, any run in the markets on the currency could obviously be cured by intervention by the central banks of all the other members, who would bail us out. The first reaction, when it was obvious the currency was now overvalued, was that we would not devalue unless the French devalued with us, but the French at that time could see no particular point in devaluing with us for the sake of it. When the inevitable run on sterling began we just expected that the Germans in particular would step in and intervene so heavily as to restore the pound to its preordained value within the ERM band. The view of the Germans on this suggestion was similar to that of the French when it was suggested that they might devalue, and the whole thing collapsed. I was left with the problem that we had run up an enormous and mounting fiscal deficit and we had promised to lower taxation as one of the key features of our economic policy.

You may gather that my own views are of those of a fiscal conservative. When I was asked what my lecture was to be about, I remembered that the aims of my chancellorship were to try to restore the reputation of our government for economic competence. I proposed to follow a fairly orthodox route of doing what every chancellor since the Second World War had tried to do, which is to produce low inflation combined with growth. It seemed to me that one important part of that equation was healthy public finances. Therefore one of the key things was to deal with the fiscal crisis I faced as rapidly as possible.

My views were straightforward: they were inherited from Geoffrey Howe to a certain extent. Nigel Lawson in particular believed that low inflation was a worthwhile aim to pursue and that you did that by the proper use of monetary policy. You set interest rates primarily with the aim of achieving low inflation, and the principal duty you had as far as tax and spending was concerned was to achieve healthy public finances. The combination of the two should create an adequate level of stability for the real economy to thrive. So I set about tackling both those things.

As far as the fiscal crisis was concerned, I decided the first thing I ought to do was to lower expectations. So, rather to the consternation of my colleagues, I went around advertising immediately after my appointment how serious the fiscal problem was, and the headlines at the time about Britain imminently heading for a £50 billion fiscal deficit in the relevant financial year were largely fostered by me, trying to make people aware of the fact that this was the immediate problem I was facing. It provided the essential background to the tough control on public spending, and the reversal of expectations of most of my colleagues, that we had to embark upon, and also to the likely tax decisions I was going to have to take as soon as I got round to delivering a budget. People who are prepared for the worst will tend to take bad news with slightly more cheerfulness. I certainly did not arrive trying to give the impression that I thought all would be for the best in the best of all possible worlds now that I had taken over. I had some modest success in lowering expectations.

I will not bore you with the details of the public spending rounds I oversaw. Our government ran an annual public spending round. It dominated the lives of most ministers. One round ran into the next. I believed that the control of public spending was one of our key duties so I threw myself into it with some enthusiasm. I had been a member of the relevant Cabinet committee practically throughout my career. I had always been at spending departments, but also found myself on the Cabinet committee that used to settle disputes between the Treasury and spending ministers – which was always known as the Star Chamber.

When I first went on it I used to go as a junior member of the Cabinet. I used to settle my own spending round with the Treasury rather early. I aimed to get in early because I did not have enough clout to drag it out too much, so I wanted to get the best settlement I could early on. I knew that one way I might get more money out of the Treasury was if they thought that my fiscal conservatism could be turned to their advantage as long as they settled with me. I used to think it was worth a few billion more on my particular budget if they settled with me early, so that I would then turn into one of the prosecuting counsel against my colleagues when it came to other people who recklessly held out late. I first appeared in the Star Chamber under Willie Whitelaw's chairmanship, when he used to get me to be a kind of prosecuting counsel on people who were so unwary as to turn up and try to get more.

By the time I arrived as chancellor the system had become even more useful, because the Cabinet committee which settled all disputes with spending departments was chaired by the chancellor of the Exchequer. At it, the chief secretary, my number 2, would present the Treasury's proposals, which would then be challenged and denounced by the spending minister. Then a discussion would take place in which both the chief secretary and the chancellor had a voice and the chancellor had the chair. So it really was judge and jury being controlled by the Treasury, and it enabled us to achieve some considerable success, particularly with Michael Portillo, who was then my chief secretary. He was a more than competent presenter of the Treasury's case and my adjudications in his favour were particularly easy to give. That was a vital part of controlling public finances, a problem which went on throughout my time.

As far as taxes were concerned, it was quite obvious to me that I was going to have to raise them. A slight difficulty, as the politically acute will recall, was that my party had insisted on fighting the 1992 election on a policy of reducing taxation. This was a constant nuisance to me throughout my period of office! In my defence I have never believed that we should have fought the 1992 election on a policy of reducing taxes. I had made it quite clear to my key colleagues that I thought it was totally irresponsible to fight the election on that basis. Some of the things that were said in the campaign were quite difficult for me as chancellor. I kept having quotations thrown at me about how we would reduce taxes year in, year out. As soon as I was appointed everybody went racing off to look for quotations from me making these propositions. Fortunately, as I had not agreed with this platform in 1992, I had never echoed it. That proved to be very useful protection.

The unfortunate voters in my own constituency of Rushcliffe, if you were to look at my election manifestos (as journalists did rather more than my constituents, I suspect), had been offered the rather deadly promise that we would put the public finances back into a healthy condition. I made no promise to anybody that we would reduce taxation. I took the view that I would believe that when I saw it, and I waited to see what would happen. So every time people found a quotation from one of my senior colleagues that they would reduce taxes year in, year out, and so on, I was able to say 'not me'.

Our national manifesto had been slightly reticent on the subject. I made a few mistakes, like being reduced to saying at one point that I would only regard myself as bound by the written manifesto and I was not going to take any more notice of stray remarks that someone had made on a wet Wednesday night in Dudley in the course of the campaign. That immediately got the Dudley newspaper pursuing me for the next month under headlines of 'Clarke says it's alright to lie in Dudley'. But I set aside the ridiculous platform we were on, and in the national interest we had to raise some revenue.

I had an extraordinary effect when I presented my first budget. Preparing that first budget was great fun. No doubt the process has been explained to you. It did not change all that much in my time compared with that of any of my four predecessors. When I prepared my first budget it took six months' hard work, and it was quite a tough budget. I decided to enjoy it. I got up and delivered it with as much élan as I could. The day of the budget is just a circus. Why the British turn it into a circus I have no idea, but in my day you waved red boxes and a great performance went on. You sipped whisky and decided that if this was your one opportunity to try to sell it you had better have a go. I was, I have to admit, full of trepidation and I was astonished when I sat down to realize there were backbenchers waving order papers and cheering. The write-ups the next morning were also good, which is always very dangerous. The worst budgets are the ones that get the immediate acclaim! I decided that nobody had been listening to a word I had been saying! I think that budget still holds the record as the largest increase in the burden of taxation in any budget delivered by any chancellor since the war, and it appeared to be greeted on all sides with only a modicum of criticism and otherwise general approval. It was a course upon which I set myself for the remainder of my time, to my eventual regret.

Let me say that my regret is that of a Conservative. Here I am speaking as a Tory, not as a chancellor. I belong to that version of the Conservative Party which used to win elections and I do on the whole have prejudices in favour of lowering the burden of taxation and controlling public expenditure. But it was not my privilege to do so for most of the time I was there. I had to keep lowering the standard rate of income tax a little and continuing to develop the lower band, because that was such an article of faith to all my backbenchers that it was necessary to nod in that direction for the purposes of presentation. Bear in mind they were all feuding against the Franco-German plot and being expelled, or losing the whip. Riots were breaking out day by day, so at least the budget had to have a little in it to encourage the more hard line of my colleagues to come with us. It did not require tremendous intellect to realize that what I was doing to the married couples' allowance, and so on, was cancelling out what I was doing on the standard rate.

The greatest excitement I ever caused to the Customs and Excise, which was not my favourite part of the department, was to invent new taxes for them. I did think that the Inland Revenue were on the whole a little more competent than Customs and Excise, but the Customs and Excise people were thrilled when I actually, with them, devised new taxes. No part of the Revenue or the Treasury had been given new taxes for a very long time. We looked at some pretty odd propositions, but what we actually came up with was the airport passenger tax, to get round the difficulty that aviation fuel pays no taxation. I introduced the insurance tax in order to tackle the way in which quite a lot of companies, particularly travel agents amongst others, were making a much bigger return on the insurance they sold because it was tax-free compared with the VATable goods and services that they sold. They were opposed at the time by my opponents. These new taxes have all been increased by my opponents once they got into office. They did a pretty good job of raising more much-needed revenue.

I have not come here to be partisan. We did look at quite a lot of things each year, analysing the budget, forming the budget judgement, realizing that we had to continue to keep the fiscal deficit narrowing towards my chosen target of a balanced budget over the cycle. We were constantly looking for forms of revenue. I remember a week or two studying an Irish tax on plastic bags which seems to work in Ireland, but I could not figure out how on earth it could possibly work in the United Kingdom. We did look at the tax treatment of pensions and at Corporation Tax. We did contemplate the possibility of abolishing dividend tax credit for pension funds. It was potentially a good little earner: £5 billion a year was not to be sneezed at. I am able to say in my defence that we looked at it and rejected it for what seemed to be a sound policy reason. You needed some preferential tax treatment of the pensions industry in order to keep up a proper level of investment in pensions in this country. So we rejected some increases, but we did get steadily on a downward path of public expenditure and, more importantly, public sector borrowing. We were on course for the tough fiscal rule that I had set for restoring the public finances to good health.

That left monetary policy and the need to get down to low inflation. That in turn involved taking a sensible view on the setting of interest rates. Now I was always in favour of having an independent Bank of England. There is nothing very complicated about the political views that people were likely to have about whether or not you need an independent central bank. It seemed to me over most of the developed world that those politicians who were right of centre tended to be in favour of having independent banks and those who were left of centre tended to be in favour of having politically controlled banks.

I do not know what they said in their lectures, but it is my firm belief that Geoffrey Howe was in favour of an independent bank, that Nigel Lawson was in favour of an independent bank, and that Norman Lamont was in favour of an independent bank. And I was in favour of having an independent bank. The slight snag was that neither of the prime ministers we served was remotely interested in having an independent bank. Indeed John Major, the chancellor I missed out, was the only chancellor we ever had who was not in favour of having an independent bank. I am not quite sure what exactly John's views were. I do remember being a minor witness of a conversation between Margaret Thatcher and Nigel Lawson when finally, in exasperation, Margaret threw her hands up and said she could not possibly have an independent bank. They might raise interest rates on the eve of an election she said, which was in her view quite unthinkable. I rapidly discovered that I was not going to get an independent bank out of my prime minister either.

What we actually did in those early days was to take advantage of the fact that I was new and able to change things, and to take advantage as well of the policy framework that we had set ourselves, to the great credit of my distinguished predecessor Norman Lamont. Norman is a friend of mine, but he did leave under something of a cloud. He was not able to recover his reputation after Black Wednesday, which is why he went. I remember, in one of my unhelpful black humour comments during the day, I remarked that I seemed to be a member of a government that had no economic policy at all. Norman had very rapidly presided over putting in place a new framework of policy based on inflation targeting, which was a pretty important step, and obviously I was committed to following that, but it did require a disciplined approach to monetary policy in order to achieve it. As I could not get an independent Bank of England I consciously moved to make the whole process more open, to try and get rid of as much of the political pressure as I possibly could on interest rate setting, and for that reason, in fairly short order, introduced one or two changes.

The first was that the Bank of England should be entitled to produce its own inflation report without editing or correction by the Treasury. The Bank of England used to produce an inflation report as a background explanation to decisions, but the Bank submitted it, and the Treasury rewrote it, in a way which they thought suited the policy of the government they served and the predilections of their chancellor. For the future the background to investment rate decisions would be an inflation report actually composed by the Bank of England, presided over by the governor, and published independently. I went so far as to allow the Governor of the Bank of England to make speeches on the subject of the macro-economic policy, particularly inflation, without having them edited by the Treasury. The governor of the Bank, I discovered, was supposed to submit drafts of speeches to me in order to warn me before he made any public statements and to enable my officials to suggest that he might remove embarrassing phrases of any kind. We abandoned that control.

Also, I decided to have regular monthly meetings at which, unless there was some crisis, interest rate decisions would be taken. I would chair them. They would also be attended by my junior ministers, which I remember caused a certain amount of concern, as junior ministers were not meant to be engaged in that kind of thing in the opinion of some corners of the Treasury. They all came along, and they had useful opinions, alongside officials of the Treasury and the governor, the deputy governor and officials of the Bank of England. There would be minutes of these meetings and after a reasonable delay they were to be published.

My aim was, firstly, to try to have an open and sensible debate about policy-making, but also to give a much higher profile to the advice I was getting from the Bank. I might not be able to have an independent Bank of England, because that was politically impossible, but the Governor of the Bank of England became a public figure. Suddenly his views were known when you read the minutes. This was most useful because, apart from anything else, heaven forbid that any political pressures were put upon me in order to adjust interest rates against the governor's advice.

The thing that irritated me most was that, when we first produced them, nobody took any notice of the minutes. Compared with most politicians, I do not often moan about the media and the press in this country. I think we get the media we deserve and that politicians get the media that they deserve. The financial press and the business press are probably the most distinguished section of the media: there are some extremely valuable commentators. But of course they all thought this was a fix, this was just a Treasury press release, and it did not represent what anybody actually said at any real meeting. This was all part of the spin, as it would now be called, so I could not get anybody to take any notice of it.

The one mistake I made at a meeting of the Treasury Select Committee was to start complaining, saying, 'I do wish people would have a look at these minutes and realize they are genuine minutes of genuine meetings. I wish they would accept that and not just regard it as the "Ken and Eddie show".' Of course, far from having the effect I intended, all I did was get the thing christened the 'Ken and Eddie show' forever thereafter.

The key thing that made people believe them was when the minutes first revealed that I had not accepted the advice of the Governor of the Bank of England and we began to disagree. Then it really did become the 'Ken and Eddie show'. We did disagree, and if you get a body of that sort together, as is true of the Monetary Policy Committee now, the idea that every time they meet every man and woman present is going to be of a unanimous opinion is implausible. It does happen in some months: sometimes it is obvious that you should not change, but every now and again opinions are bound to diverge. As far as I can recall, Eddie and I never got more than 25 basis points apart, and only people such as Mervyn King or Howard Davies were ever great outliers. We were roughly in the same direction.

I used to object to their heavy reliance on the Bank of England's computer model of the economy and the way it was going, for which I did not have as much regard as they did. I had just the same disregard for the Treasury's computer model. It did seem to me that it just factored in what had happened when things had gone wrong before. Whatever goes wrong in macro-economic policy the irritating thing is that it is never the same thing twice. But in those days in the mid-1990s there was a constant fear, amongst those with more experience of economic policy-making than I had, that we were about to have huge inflationary pressures. Whenever prices started picking up we were obviously going back to an inflationary wage–price cycle which you would eventually have to correct. I steadily came to believe that these inflationary pressures just were not as strong as some of my extremely distinguished advisers believed.

The differences of view which did emerge on rates, and which were never substantial, did not arise for political reasons. We had reached the stage where it seemed to me that you got as much credit for putting rates up as for putting them down, as long as you persuaded people you were doing it for reputable, responsible reasons, to create the right climate for the steady recovery from the recession which was taking place.

I will say a few words on another topic that is outside the subject matter that I agreed to cover. The other thing that dominated my life was the euro and preparations for the euro. I am hesitant to go into this because I am now regarded as associated, if nothing else, with European politics in this country. If ever I go anywhere and some local journalist is interviewing me and cannot think what to ask, they ask me first about the current leader of the Conservative Party, because we always have a leadership crisis, so I always avoid that, and then they ask me about Europe.

I do not mind being associated with Europe. I am extremely pro-European, I am as pro-European as practically all Conservatives were when I first joined the party, and I have not changed my mind in any way. I was in favour of the single currency, but then we were all in favour of the single currency until it got near to reality. I think I am more particularly associated with Europe than most other people because I happened to be the chancellor who went along to Ecofin at a time when the rules of the single currency were being worked out. This was a long and elaborate process. It was fascinating. I was in principle in favour of a single currency just as I am in favour of a single market, and I thought if we could ever get enough of the economies to be sustainably convergent then a single market would work better with a single means of exchange, so I was quite happy to go along with it.

The Maastricht Treaty had been quite well written, and the so-called Maastricht Rules that we all had to achieve in order to become candidates for membership of the single currency struck me as no more than common sense. I used to defend them to my colleagues, saying, if they ever had a Conservative chancellor who did not believe that you ought to strive to keep the fiscal deficit below 3 per cent of GDP and not have the total sum of national debt above 60 per cent of GDP, well, they did not have a Conservative chancellor, this is all prudent economics. So I got heavily involved as well in the preparations for the currency.

I can remember two particular crises. The first was when the whole thing nearly collapsed. I had only been in office for about twelve months. Despite the French bravado at the time of the ERM, the time soon came when the strong franc was under pressure and was going through exactly the same speculative run against it as we were. Crisis meetings were held in Brussels to try to decide what to do about the ERM when the French and several of the other currencies seemed likely to drop out of the bottom of the band. That was a fascinating evening, one of the most interesting meetings I have ever attended. It was never reported here, because we had reached the stage when the reporting that came back from Brussels, Ecofin, the Council of Finance Ministers, bore absolutely no relationship to what we were talking about. The readers of the *Daily Telegraph* could always read some version of the Franco-German plot which I was invariably fighting, but it did not normally concern the actual subject matter of the day.

We did have a fascinating evening. A tremendous row broke out, at which I was a bit of a spectator because we were not in the ERM. It concerned mainly the ERM members, but I was an interested spectator and I got on well with my colleagues, and I spent my time eating French baguettes and drinking a little wine and a little water as they all went off in bilaterals which got nowhere. Eventually they all came back and said that no agreement could be reached, so we were going to wait to see what the markets did to the franc in the morning. So having spent an evening doing little in particular, I decided to start intervening and gave them a very long speech about the path on which we were set and the disastrous consequences of giving up. What on earth was going to happen when it was all taken apart in the morning? Was the whole thing to be upended by one day's turmoil in the markets?

I do not think my intervention was crucial – though Jean-Claude Trichet always says it was – it just gained us a few more minutes. Then the German Finance Minister got on to Helmut Kohl, and the French Finance Minister got on the phone to François Mitterrand, and they were firmly told in blunter language than I had used that they had got to go back and sort this out. For a while it looked as though they were going to abandon the European single currency and the Maastricht criteria. But we came up with a solution which would have helped the British the year before. We decided that the franc should be allowed to fluctuate within a 15 per cent band, in other words a band so wide it was meaningless. As a result the whole thing continued with the rules satisfactorily intact and amended, and we returned to our labours meeting by meeting.

The other really interesting meeting was in Dublin when we agreed the Stability and Growth Pact. I still defend the Stability and Growth Pact. It was a good way of entrenching the Maastricht criteria, as it were, apart from the fines. The idea that recalcitrant governments were going to be fined struck me as pretty dotty, but it was absolutely insisted upon by the Germans, perversely, who did not trust the Italians. So they wanted to threaten to fine the Italians if, as usual, they got back into an unsustainable deficit situation that went above 3 per cent. Everybody got very heated about this because it had become absolutely non-negotiable for the Germans. The problem was that the President of the Bundesbank, a very powerful figure who had been persuaded by Helmut Kohl to go along with the single currency, had decided this was his last-ditch stand. If they had to throw in their lot with some European central bank which would not be like the Bundesbank, you had to make sure at least it wasn't undermined by the Italians. So they insisted on the fine.

It all got completely out of hand. I remember standing very close and watching agitated conversation, angry conversation, fists waving about, red faces between Helmut Kohl and Jacques Chirac, arguing about who was going to give way on the stability pact and the fines. It was not helped by the fact that they did not have a language in common. It also, in my modest opinion, was not helped by the fact that neither of them had the first idea of what was really beneath the argument. Both were being egged on by their respective finance ministers and central bank governors. But in the end common sense prevailed, and we agreed the Stability and Growth Pact. We did agree the fines, but all expected that nobody in their right mind would ever try to levy them.

I can only claim to have made one personal contribution to the euro. My colleagues were all sympathetic with me since I was dealing with these lunatic journalists who kept going back and giving weird accounts of our meetings, reporting on the end of Britain as an independent nation and the destruction of our control over our own tax and public spending system. I had to have something to get the *Daily Mail* and the *Daily Telegraph* off my back, so we did make an issue of the design of the coins and notes. It could not affect the notes because the governors insisted that central banks did notes, and the governors of the banks chose dreadful architectural anonymous designs which are now all over the euro notes. But I decided it would cheer up my more passionate nationalist opinion at home if it was possible to have a national symbol on the coins.

I must admit by this stage I realized there was not a snowball's chance in Hades of the British being amongst the first joiners, but one day it will be useful to be able to tell my doubting fellow citizens that the queen's head would indeed gaze out at them if they actually had a euro. Oh, this was impossible, various people were produced to say. You cannot have different coins in the same jurisdiction. I remember I got my people to take over a whole collection of British coins to show that our pound coins did have different things on one side. I did not tell them that hardly any Englishmen know that they have got different things on one side and it did not matter a two-penny damn what was on as long as it was difficult to forge the coins. Eventually, it was only down to the sympathy my colleagues had for the situation I was placed in, with these dreadful journalists waiting like wolves outside the door to find another sacrifice in the national interest that I was making, that we had the euro coins with a national symbol on one side.

So when you go to Europe you will find different designs. The only real problem was with the Spanish minister. It took a long time to explain to him that it would not be as difficult as he thought it would be, because he thought if you had different sides on the coins you would have to return them all to their country of origin every time they were used. He thought the cost of train loads of euro coins going to and fro would be immense. I explained slowly that we did not return the Scottish ones to Scotland or the Irish ones to Ireland, and actually in London if he looked at his pound coins he would find thistles and all kinds of things on them.

Alas, as far as Britain was concerned, it was all in vain – although I am not sure we ever had a moment when we could ideally have joined the euro and could be confident we were sustainably convergent. But we will one day. It was worthwhile work because I think we have a successful currency in Europe, and it does improve the workings of the single market where it circulates.

The worst mistake I ever made in politics was to allow John Major to persuade Heseltine and me that we should have a referendum on whether to join the single currency. I have no time for referendums, and to have a referendum on your monetary policy is an extremely strange way of running a modern industrial state. I have not gone back on the deal, having agreed to it, so I will have to go through with it, and to take part. But of course it has produced eight years of paralysing inactivity with nobody able to take any decision whatever on the subject, and it does look likely to last yet further.

I will defend my record. At the moment, we have had twelve years of growth with low inflation of a kind not achieved in the United Kingdom at any time, I think in history Gordon now says, certainly in modern times. I always point out that the first four years were mine, and I also say they were the difficult bit. He did not take over the background I did of economic crisis and slow emergence from a recession.

When we came to fight the election the feel-good factor was at the level the pollsters said was necessary for governments to win elections. The outlook that people had as far as their economic well-being was concerned was reasonable. We had won back our reputation for economic competence and were now beginning to inch ahead of the Labour Party in that area, so I wanted to fight the election on the economy. But two things thwarted me. One was that all my colleagues thought the election had to be about Europe, just as they did in 2001, and the other thing was that Tony and Gordon decided that the best way to stop me going on about the economy was to say they agreed with me. So they said they would not increase taxation. That surprised me. I would have done it if I had needed to, but they said they would not raise rates, they would not change the National Insurance thresholds on public expenditure, they would stick to my figures – indeed they stuck to my figures in spades. They turned one of our three-year settlements into a three-year unadjustable settlement: it was eye-watering.

It was rather difficult to fight against an opposition who just said they would carry on doing what we did before. Gordon Brown even echoed my speeches about the euro to the word, and the election was fought on other things. So I happily claimed to my own satisfaction at least that the complete rout which we suffered was nothing particularly to do with me. Indeed, had we stuck with the economy we might have done very much better.

I hope I have given you at least a perspective on the years I was at the Treasury. I have probably glided over all the detail which an academic audience will be anxious to press me on, but I hope at least I leave you with a message that I am unrepentant and that I certainly enjoyed it. It was the best job I ever had.

Questions and Answers

Since Gordon Brown became chancellor your party has manifestly struggled to find someone who matches him. None of the several Conservative shadow chancellors who have shadowed him have ever really laid a glove on him. For example, William Hague watched his three successive shadow chancellors, Peter Lilley, Francis Maude and your friend Michael Portillo,

get slaughtered by Brown. Even the current shadow chancellor, Oliver Letwin, is not doing much better. He was widely praised when he was shadowing the Home Secretary, David Blunkett, but when he took over shadowing the chancellor, Gordon Brown started sawing him up in the House of Commons. Why do you think that it is? Is that because the economy is doing so well that your party cannot find the answer, or is it just because your parliamentary party is so short on talent like you? You cannot find someone who matches Gordon Brown.

It is quite obvious I don't agree with every precondition you set in your question! Firstly, apart from anything else you've missed out Michael Howard. I think Michael Howard rebuilt his political reputation by being an extremely formidable shadow chancellor. He'd been on the front bench, then he had gone out, then he came back, and as shadow chancellor he was head and shoulders above the members of the shadow front bench, and I think Howard was perfectly capable of holding his own with Gordon Brown.

Otherwise you have answered your question yourself. It was extremely difficult to be opposite him at a time when the economy was doing so well. By the time he took over, the economy was doing well and it continued to do better. He did not wreck the economy, he did do what he promised to do as far as tax and spending was concerned, and quite apart from the fact that the world economy was on an up at first and we were coming out of recession, he then went into a period where we had an

American-led boom which turned out to be an unhealthy boom. For a time the economy began to do roaringly well and their rhetoric constantly harped on our history of recession. Most of the comparisons they make go back to the 1980s rather than the 1990s in fact. We are always having hurled at us accusations about high inflation rates and so on, but the rates they quote are not the ones they took over, they are ones they pluck out of the air from the hyper-inflationary era throughout the world of the 1980s.

Gordon was walking on water until about two or three years ago with the real economy thriving. I think he is heading for a fall and I don't agree that Oliver is losing the argument now. Since Brown has ceased to be prudent, since he became 'tax and spend', he has become extremely complacent, and the British public are extremely complacent about the state of our economy. The public on the whole I fear are persuaded that somehow we have the finest performing economy in the world, free of problems. Everybody else has problems which we don't have. Most of the British think we have the fastest growing economy in Europe, which you know is not the case, but they all think it is. They think we have the lowest levels of unemployment and all the rest of it, so it is still quite difficult for the opposition. But we are getting the argument across that Gordon Brown has increased the burden of taxation to no worthwhile effect, that the levels of public expenditure are now somewhat out of control, and the total level of public expenditure is getting excessive and isn't producing any noticeable improvement in public services, or not enough improvement to show value for money so far as the tax payer is concerned.

The idea that he is sitting on some very uncertain fiscal rules so that, if he wins an election, he will have to increase the burden of taxation yet further simply to cope with what he himself has created by his public spending plans of the last few years, all those are quite good things to get across. Our case at the moment is not that we can reduce taxes in a hurry, but to say that if you don't do something about public spending you are going to have to increase taxes. The argument about the tax increases Gordon Brown will undoubtedly have to bring in is a good one. I also think the British are steadily losing their competitive position, that our present growth rate is based on dangerous levels of both public and household debt, and that it is not guaranteed to be sustainable for very much longer. All of those are perfectly valid points. But what I was trying to argue against Gordon in the first three or four years was almost impossible because there was a Labour honeymoon and the economy was going on in a fairly untroubled fashion. I think that is the real answer to your question.

Gordon wasn't great shakes as a shadow chancellor. But he has become a good debater, better than he was. He wasn't much good in the House of Commons. He used to produce great, rather content-free, shopping lists. He used to get up and demand a strategy for invest-ment and a strategy for growth and a strategy for jobs. He still goes on in a non-stop recitative which you cannot interrupt. He's better than he was but I think he is getting more and more vulnerable.

As chancellor did you find it a help or a hindrance to have around the prime minister a group of advisers who might be giving different advice from the advice coming from the Treasury?

I didn't actually suffer from that. The prime minister's advisers of the day are always a blessed nuisance to some minister or another, but John did not take on board any really maverick advisers on the economy. He had political advisers but not influential ones who took the view, which political advisers to prime ministers always do, that taxes are things that only go down and that interest rates are things that only go down, but there wasn't anybody he took particular notice of. There was no Alan Walters for me to contend with. There wasn't really anybody who had strong views on economic policy and other areas of policy. At times advisers can be perfectly helpful and useful, but occasionally prime ministers do get inclined to take on board swivel-eyed young men with great think-tank ideas who are a nuisance if you are trying to implement policy. Fortunately none of them were actually in my field and John didn't have that type of entourage. His advisers were very, very keen and they used to intervene occasionally, getting him to commit himself to the abolition of Inheritance Tax and the abolition of Capital Gains Tax, but fortunately as this was a timeless commitment I was able to say, alright, we would address that problem when the opportunity arose. It never actually arose! I don't know whether it is still our policy or not.

You said that the Stability and Growth Pact is an important part of the package surrounding the euro, and you also pointed out, as we've all noticed, that it has got no teeth. If it is important to have it, but it has got no teeth, how would you reshape it in order for it to work better?

I wouldn't reshape it very much. I have some sympathy with Gordon's argument that in addressing a government that is breaching one of those provisions you should have some regard to the overall position, like the total level of debt in relation to GDP.

One of the achievements of the finance ministers in the 1990s, who at G7 level were all achieving a quite remarkable level of consensus, was to get back to an altogether more responsible view of fiscal policy. Sound public finances and low inflation were actually the policies being pursued by just about every finance minister I ever met, certainly in the United States. People like Bob Rubin were entirely in accord on that.

The 1980s had been a terrible time of deficit-led government so, through most of the 1990s, in most countries in the Western world, you had finance ministers crawling back to more common sense and fiscal responsibility. The Maastricht Treaty was a very useful benchmark. For most of the Europeans it was very useful, because they could say to their political colleagues that they had to get their fiscal deficit down to comply with Maastricht. My own party, however, hated Maastricht. I had to say, 'You've got the fiscal deficit down, but of course it has nothing to do with Maastricht!' As it happens Maastricht is common sense anyway. Maastricht is what we should follow as a Conservative government.

One of the big successes of EMU was achieved by the discipline that was self-imposed by the governments in the run-up to the euro so they could all qualify. It did get the level of fiscal deficits in Western Europe in order. But this is all a political thing: it isn't a federal superstate, it is a union of states. It is a permanent process of negotiation and horse-trading, and the way in which you influence the behaviour of others is just argument, persuasion, or the threat of publicity in order to get people to adhere to a reasonably solid core of policy. We have mutual surveillance of economic policy. We produce targets for each other. Everybody is now wildly excited that the new treaty has all this stuff which I have heard David Heathcoat-Amory say means we will not have a British budget. I pointed out he was in the Treasury with me when we were complying with these rules. They are Maastricht, but they are quite sensible rules. It is quite a good discipline actually to have a review, a mutual surveillance of what you're doing, and to agree some targets.

If a government is going out of line, if there is some good reason for it, all the pact demands is that the government should address the problem and be seen to be taking some action to try to get back into balance. The only problem arises if you ever have a totally recalcitrant government that has gone back to some former approach to policy and thought this is all a bankers' ramp and it is necessary to spend whatever you had to spend in response to your different political lobbies.

If they were threatening the stability of the whole you'd have to throw them out, but the present German Finance Minister has always said he is going to abide by the stability pact, the French Finance Minister said he's going to abide by the stability pact. Their political heads of government, who are not strong on this front, occasionally come out with strange remarks, but actually it does confine their deficit and they are going to get back within it. Peer pressure, publicity, particularly in Germany, will have an effect. No German Finance Minister can appear totally irresponsible to the German population, who place very, very high importance on the stability of their currency and the soundness of their public finances. No Frenchman dare either.

The problem at the moment is that the threat of penalties raised the problem to a level of crisis because the penalties all keep getting turned over and not applied. So the reaction is that all the major countries are now trying to find some way of bending the rules and weakening them. The only reason the French and Germans are outside the pact and we're outside the terms of the pact, though we are not in the euro, is fiscal irresponsibility in the run-up to elections. There is no macroeconomic reason. The present levels of the German deficit, the French deficit or indeed the British deficit are too high. A bit of peer pressure gives a counterweight politically to push people back inside. That's how it ought to work.

In the light of your remarks, what do you think about Gordon Brown selling off the gold reserves for euros?

I always wanted to sell the gold reserves. I never could understand why our reserves had gold in them. You do need to have some reserves, and in my opinion they should be held in a basket of currencies from those nations with which you do most of your trade. That's the obvious basis of reserves, and I couldn't understand why we had gold. It is very good for jewellery, otherwise it only has mystique dating back to the time of the pharaohs. I had some rather entertaining meetings because the Bank was quite keen on gold at the time, and some bank officials were wheeled in to try to stop the chancellor talking about selling gold. It was mainly for light entertainment, part of my running a permanent debating society, that I asked them why we needed gold, and I used to argue against some of the reasons that were put up which I didn't think had much substance. I can remember the one that they all used to fall back on was, 'Chancellor, if we ever have a third world war it might be the only means of exchange upon which we could fall back.' I thought that if we had a third world war there would be bigger problems than that.

I can only say that if I had sold gold I hope I would not have advertised in advance that I was going to sell it. I hope I wouldn't have been as unlucky as Gordon in judging the time when he did it. But although the gold price is now going through the roof, my off-the-cuff guess would be that gold is still not back to the level it had, say, in 1980. Over the years it has been a declining non-performing asset and in my opinion is only held in the reserves of national banks for mystical, out-of-date reasons.

You've mentioned your antipathy towards referendums, but I wondered how you will campaign on the referendum on the constitution for Europe. I presume you're in favour of that, and if the referendum is lost what do you think Britain's place in Europe would be, say, in five years' time?

I will be campaigning, if and when we ever have a referendum on the constitution, in favour of the constitution. Presupposing that most of the other countries have ratified then I think we will have to have a referendum, and I shall be campaigning for the present treaty. I hesitate launching into an answer to a question with my reasons for being in favour of this constitution, but it seems to me a necessary improvement in the way the Union works, following the recent enlargement which is one of the most significant events that has taken place in the life of the Union. I don't believe it has any adverse effects of the type that are claimed. It doesn't affect our criminal justice system. It does improve the way you can enforce the fight against international cross-border crime. The main extension is in the area of immigration and asylum policy, where it seems to me twenty-five national policies have plainly failed, most particularly that of the United Kingdom. So I would wish to have a supernational European approach to the problems of movement of peoples which everybody wants to be effective, but I hope that everyone would want to be reasonably liberal and humane in such a policy as well. So I will be campaigning for a yes vote.

What will happen if we vote no? Well, I think you should ask one of the people against the treaty that. One of the weaknesses of the people who say they are going to vote no seems to me that they haven't got the first idea what happens if we vote no. They actually disagree among themselves. Mr Kilroy Silk is no doubt very happily saying, well, you just leave, but the ones who claim that they disagree with Mr Kilroy Silk seem to me a bit hard pressed. They say no, we just stay with the treaties we've got and you try and run the twenty-five on the basis of constitutional treaties we already have. That may happen if one of the others rejects it, but I think the treaties we have are inadequate.

If any of the others reject it, it won't be for British reasons. I recently met Laurent Fabius, the French socialist who is causing all the trouble and trying to get the French socialists to vote against it. I asked him, 'What on earth are you doing? You make me look like a Eurosceptic. You've been extremely pro-European all your life – is this not European enough?' He greatly objects to this union of nation-states which has been created. This treaty is called in France 'La Britannique' and so will cause confusion. My main worry is it will cause mayhem inside the Union, with a particular crisis about what the Britain's relationship is with the rest. I don't think it would lead to our leaving the community, but it could certainly lead to us being marginalized and to a great deal of pressure from our enemies to try to remove us to associate status, which is not satisfactory for the Norwegians, for the Icelanders or for the Leichtensteiners and would not be for us. It would remove us from influence in the next stages of the treaty.

Of course there are those who say that a no vote will cause others to agree to start renegotiating all the treaties back to 1972. That is preposterous. Here you have twenty-five nation-states who just agreed a constitutional fabric for a union which ten of them are particularly eager to join, and if the British say no, apparently you get down to a renegotiation so the British can have their fish back and their aid money back and not have to join the social chapter. They have got to get twenty-four nation-states to agree. Those who are saying they should vote no had better think of a better argument than that about what the consequences are going to be if they succeed. But of course it might never be held. If you carry on pushing things off, they never quite occur.

You were reported, correctly or not, as having boasted that you had never read the Maastricht Treaty. Would you make the same boast about the constitutional treaty? If you have read it, do you understand it? If you do, you are a better person than most constitutional lawyers I have met.

I will not wax indignant about all this stuff about my not having read the Maastricht Treaty, which I can never shrug off: these things follow you to your grave. Norman Tebbit is a shrewd operator, and what I hadn't read was the text he had got hold of which showed all the corrections to the previous treaties. The version he'd got was Page 2, Paragraph 3, delete and insert part. He hadn't read it; nobody had read it.

I am perfectly familiar with the combined treaty which people like you and I always use, which I had to use as a working document when I was chancellor. I took part in the debates on the Maastricht Treaty. My own claim was that I knew the Maastricht Treaty a damn sight better than any other Member of Parliament I'd met because I had to use it more, and most of the anti-Maastricht campaigners who were going so hysterical about it in the 1990s cannot now remember why they were against it. If you look up the more preposterous claims they made, which are most of the preposterous claims being repeated now, none of them happened. Every treaty I have ever defended, from the Treaty of Accession onwards, I have been told the monarch will be removed, our taxes will go up, we'll lose control over our public spending, and all these vast numbers of shoeless foreigners will come here spreading disease and taking our jobs. And it has never happened, and there is nothing in the present treaty to make that happen either.

I have read the present treaty. It is hard work. It has only very recently been available. I don't think many other Members of Parliament have, because if you ask for it at the Vote Office of the House of Commons you cannot get a copy. I don't think they're flooded with demand – you've really got to fish around a bit to find a copy of this treaty. It is as readable as most legal texts are, and in the course of my much reshuffled career I think I have attended more Council of Ministers meetings on every conceivable subject than most people have had hot dinners, because I was attending them from 1979 onwards. Whenever I had a Cabinet boss it was one who didn't want to go to Brussels to attend Council meetings, so I have always attended Council of Ministers meetings until my masters the public threw me out of office altogether, so I reckon I did understand it.

I don't fondly imagine the referendum will be about the content of the treaty. The thing about referendums is they're a lottery. The public never answer the question they're asked. Nobody's ever going to go down to the detail of the textual analysis of the treaty. It is eye-glazing to the average audience. Whether or not we join will all depend on how the British are currently feeling about foreigners, their then prime minister, the government and other things. It is in the lap of the gods, as these referendum things always are.

Afterword

Howard Davies

In the eighteen months which have elapsed since the chancellors told their tales, in one sense we might conclude that little has changed. The inflation target regime remains in place and intact. Inflation has continued to be comfortably within the prescribed band, and Mervyn King has still not been obliged to display his letter-writing skills.

At the other end of town, Gordon Brown is still in position, now as the longest serving chancellor of modern times. There have been changes in his team. Nick McPherson has taken over from Gus O'Donnell as permanent secretary and, after a short intermission, during which he secured election to the House of Commons and served a brief apprenticeship on the back benches, Ed Balls is back as economic secretary, or 'deputy chancellor', as he has been known in Treasury Chambers for almost a decade.

The economy has continued to expand, at around its trend growth rate. The UK has now seen fifty-seven consecutive quarters of growth, a quite remarkably long period of consistent expansion, particularly when set against the chequered record of the three previous decades.

Internationally, the UK's policy regime has attracted more supporters. The number of countries adopting inflation targets has continued to grow. And even in the United States Alan Greenspan's replacement as chairman of the Federal Reserve, Ben Bernanke, has spoken and written positively about inflation targetry, though he has not so far sought to introduce this alien plant into Washington.

Far more controversy surrounds European economic and monetary union, however. After six years of the single currency, the European Central Bank has acquired a solid reputation for the control of inflation overall in the Eurozone. And the presidential transition from Wim Duisenberg to Jean Claude Trichet was smooth. But growth in countries within the Eurozone remains surprisingly divergent, and those divergences are proving, against expectations, to be persistent. Ireland has grown by 6.3 per cent a year on average for the last six years, while Italy and Germany have averaged little more than 1 per cent. Even more interestingly, there have been significant changes in competitiveness. Unit labour costs in Germany have fallen by around 7 per cent since 1999, while in Portugal they have risen by some 15 per cent. These divergences are imposing strains on the system. In Italy, where the economy remains very sluggish, there have even been calls by senior politicians for withdrawal from the Eurozone.

The Stability and Growth Pact has proved a fragile underpinning to fiscal discipline in the single currency zone, and has effectively been abandoned, in spite of a rearguard action by the European Commission. The 'no' results in the French and Dutch referenda have raised political doubts about the future of the European project as a whole. The net effect of these changes has been to make the euro seem even less attractive as a policy option for the United Kingdom. The probabilities of British adoption of the euro in the next decade have moved from very small to vanishingly tiny.

So, in terms of the debate on anti-inflation policy regimes in the UK, which is the prime subject of this volume, have we indeed reached 'the end of history'?

We cannot be sure of that, by any means. Inflation targeting does not abolish the business cycle, and at some point the new regime will need to cope with a recession. Mervyn King himself has warned that we cannot be confident in the stability of the new arrangements until they have been tested in more difficult economic conditions. At present, growth looks set to continue, and the global economic prospect is relatively benign, but, as always, there are clouds on the horizon. The government's fiscal deficit is larger than is comfortable at this stage of the cycle, and the balance of payments deficit remains worrying. Some analysts believe that, without a significant downward adjustment in the exchange rate, we are unlikely to see an improvement in the UK's external position and that deficits on the current scale are unsustainable. A significant exchange rate adjustment would pose a challenge for the Monetary Policy Committee.

It is also fair to point out that the regime has currently been operated under one chancellor only, and some aspects of the arrangements are highly personalized. Appointments to the Monetary Policy Committee are made without any clear process, and apparently on the whim of the chancellor. In a recent appearance before the Treasury Select Committee Mervyn King has made it clear that he is unhappy with this arrangement, and would prefer more systematic and transparent appointment procedures, as is the case with most other senior public positions in Britain today. A better organized process might help to avoid the gaps in the ranks of the Monetary Policy Committee which have been allowed to open up in the last year as replacements for departing members have not been found in time to keep the committee at full strength.

It seems probable, too, that during the next twelve months there will be a transition at the Treasury. Gordon Brown's expectation, and indeed the expectation of most of the country, is that he will move next door in Downing Street sometime in the coming year. If and when that happens, who will replace him in the Treasury? Would that individual be as adept at operating within the new policy framework as Gordon Brown himself has been? Will Gordon Brown as prime minister be as happy with the implications of the new regime as he was as chancellor – given that one consequence of the new structure is the exclusion of the prime minister from influence over interest rate decisions?

Until these questions are resolved, however skilful the Bank of England may be in fulfilling its remit, there will continue to be doubts about the regime's sustainability. The next two years will, therefore, be a testing time.

Appendix: Schedules

Prime Ministers

1974   1976   1979   1990   1997   Present

Harold WILSON: February 1974–March 1976

James CALLAGHAN: April 1976–May 1979

Margaret THATCHER: May 1979–November 1990

John MAJOR: November 1990–May 1997

Tony BLAIR: May 1997–Present

Chancellors of the Exchequer

| 1974 | 1979 | 1983 | 1989 | 1990 | 1993 | 1997 | Present |

Denis HEALEY: March 1974–May 1979

Sir Geoffrey HOWE: May 1979–June 1983

Nigel LAWSON: June 1983–October 1989

John MAJOR: October 1989–November 1990

Norman LAMONT: November 1990–May 1993

Kenneth CLARKE: May 1993–May 1997

Gordon BROWN: May 1997–Present

Chief Secretaries to the Treasury (1)

1974　1979　1981　1983　1985　1987　1989　1990　　Present

Tom BOARDMAN: January 1974–March 1974

Joel BARNETT: March 1974–May 1979

John BIFFEN: May 1979–January 1981

Leon BRITTAN: January 1981–June 1983

Peter REES: June 1983–September 1985

John MACGREGOR: September 1985–June 1987

John MAJOR: June 1987–July 1989

Norman LAMONT: July 1989–November 1990

David MELLOR: November 1990–April 1992

Chief Secretaries to the Treasury (2)

1992 1994 1995 1997 1998 1999 2002 2005 Present

Michael PORTILLO: April 1992–July 1994

Jonathan AITKEN: July 1994–July 1995

William WALDEGRAVE: July 1995–May 1997

Alistair DARLING: May 1997–July 1998

Stephen BYERS: July 1998–December 1998

Alan MILBURN: December 1998–October 1999

Andrew SMITH: October 1999–May 2002

Paul BOATENG: May 2002–May 2005

Des BROWNE: May 2005–May 2006

Stephen TIMMS: May 2006–Present

Permanent Secretaries to the Treasury

1974   1983   1991   1998   2002   2005   Present

Douglas WASS: July 1974–April 1983

Sir Peter MIDDLETON: April 1983–May 1991

Sir Terry BURNS: May 1991–June 1998

Sir Andrew TURNBULL: June 1998–June 2002

Sir Gus O'DONNELL: July 2002–August 2005

Nicholas MACPHERSON: August 2005–Present

Bank of England Governors

1973 1983 1993 2003 Present

Gordon RICHARDSON: *July 1973–June 1983*

Robin LEIGH-PEMBERTON : *July 1983–June 1993*

Edward GEORGE: *July 1993–June 2003*

Merryn KING: *July 2003–Present*